Capital Markets & Strategic Advisory

Investor Relations, Valuation, and the Frameworks that Shape Equity Value

By:

Zack Mukewa

Zack Mukewa

Capital markets, corporate finance and investment strategy leader with more than two decades of experience working with companies, investors and governments on IPOs, mergers and acquisitions, capital structure and funding decisions, shareholder situations and sovereign competitiveness agendas across North America, Europe, Latin America, Africa and Asia Pacific.

A practical guide for boards, executives and public policy makers in volatile markets who need to convert credibility into valuation and more reliable access to capital.

Dedication

To my parents, Peter and Dinah, whose example and discipline shaped how I see the world.

To Mbula, whose consistency, belief, and encouragement anchor more than this work.

To my son, Zayne, whose future gives this work its purpose.

Acknowledgement

This book reflects the work and thinking of many people whose names do not appear on the cover.

I am grateful to the colleagues and mentors I have worked with across finance, business and public life, whose judgment and example have shaped how I think and work. Their questions, disagreements and constraints helped turn early ideas into practical frameworks.

I would like to thank the leadership teams, boards, investors and policy makers who allowed me into the room for key moments around earnings, transactions, crises, restructurings and policy choices. The conversations and decisions in those settings sit behind much of what is in these pages.

The material has also been used and refined in workshops and sessions with executives and industry practitioners. Their feedback and examples helped sharpen the arguments and tools.

Several examples draw on real situations. Details have been anonymized, adapted or combined where necessary to protect confidentiality while keeping the core lessons intact.

I am also thankful to the editors, proofreaders and production teams involved in turning a working manuscript into a finished book. Any errors or omissions that remain are mine alone.

About The Author

Zack Mukewa has more than twenty years of experience across capital markets, corporate finance and investment strategy. He has worked with public and private companies, investors and sovereigns on IPOs, mergers and acquisitions, capital structure decisions, shareholder activism, restructurings, crises and long term competitiveness agendas across North America, Europe, Latin America, Africa and Asia Pacific.

His work centres on how capital is raised, allocated and priced. He has advised boards, CEOs, CFOs, investment committees and policy makers on valuation, funding and portfolio choices, risk and liquidity, and the design of investor and stakeholder architectures that support durable value creation. His approach combines fundamental analysis, valuation models and transaction economics with a clear view of how investors form and revise beliefs over time.

Zack has built and led capital markets and strategic advisory businesses and held leadership roles with responsibility for strategy, P&L and teams. He has worked across industries, from financial and real economy companies to technology, infrastructure and public institutions, with a focus on guiding organizations through periods of growth, transition and complexity.

𝕏: @Zackfolio

f: @Zackfolio

: @Zackfolio

: @Zackfolio

[in]: @Zackfolio

: @Zackmukewa

Table of Contents

Part I.
Foundations

Chapter 1.
Why Markets Listen

Capital markets are filled with noise. Each quarter, thousands of companies report earnings. Countless press releases, filings, and analyst notes compete for attention. Only a small fraction of this information breaks through. Investors cannot listen to everyone. They decide who matters, whose disclosures are credible, and which securities deserve their limited time and focus.

Listening in markets is not random. It is shaped by three interdependent forces: attention, trust, and liquidity. While each is a separate economic force, they are sequential in nature. Attention is the gateway. Trust increases value. Liquidity is the visible marker of confidence. When viewed together, they help understand why some companies get valuation discounts despite robust fundamentals.

1. The Economy of Attention in Capital Markets

1.1. Scarcity of Attention

Investors' attention is scarce. A portfolio manager might hold hundreds of names across funds, but a serious amount of analytical effort goes into probably a few dozen. Analysts have coverage lists, but conviction research usually boils down to half or fewer of these names. The rest are given passive attention: updates by peer readthroughs, shortcuts in the models, or just moving numbers around the earnings release.

This creates a hierarchy of who gets the attention. Large-cap issuers get attention because of scale and benchmark weighting. Their price moves drive benchmark returns, so active bets against them can translate into career risk for portfolio managers. These larger companies get sustained attention. Smaller issuers get attention only if they can create relevance to wider and larger themes.

1.2. Relevance to Borrow Attention

Attention can be borrowed when management dresses a company's narrative in the language of the forces investors are already tracking. Consider a mid-cap financial institution in Latin America with solid fundamentals but little foreign interest. International investors largely ignored it until management positioned the bank as a listed proxy for consumer credit reform. Investors already had thematic bandwidth allocated to that reform narrative. Once the bank became the investable expression of the story, attention followed.

This is a process. When we counsel companies that find it difficult to garner attention, our first question is: What three macro or sector currents are these investors following that intersect with this business (if any)? If there are none, attention needs to be established through education, which basically means it's expensive and time-consuming. If there is one, then you need to reframe the equity story and present the company as a vehicle to express the thesis.

1.3. Maintaining Attention

Borrowed attention is fragile. Without disciplined disclosure and consistent execution, initial relevance fades fast. Sustained attention requires a disclosure architecture that teaches investors how to underwrite and model the business.

For instance, in consumer categories, investors often watch companies that help them corroborate broader demand trends. A retailer that consistently discloses traffic, ticket, and mix becomes a proxy for consumer health. At that point, it can sustain attention beyond its size because it remains relevant. A retailer that cannot, or chooses not to, maintain those metrics can be pushed out of deep coverage, even when the underlying numbers are compelling.

The point is clear. Results rarely guarantee attention. Attention is engineered by relevance, and maintained by consistency.

1.4. Trust as a Multiple of Valuation

1.4.1. Regarding a Variable of Belief

Attention gets an investor meeting. Trust shapes whether investors act on what they read. In the absence of trust, even compelling numbers are sheared off. In the presence of trust, investors allow companies leeway in difficult times.

Trust is evident in market data. A narrow consensus range expresses a high degree of trust in the guidance. A wide range suggests a lack of trust in management's ability to follow through. Coverage notes distill the question of whether management's words are sticky or just puffery. Investors may not state the role of trust as a driver of value, but it's built into their models.

1.4.2. How Analysts Build Trust in Their Work

In practice, analysts apply "haircuts" to management guidance. A company that misses targets consistently may have a haircut on its forecasts of 10-30%, before they even hit the output of the model. Another sign of value economics flows from peer grouping. Analysts implicitly determine which companies' "merit" to be compared to leaders or laggards – this is therefore reputational, not mathematical.

A European industrial company with strong growth, but poor governance, earned its place among weaker peers. The result was a valuation of two to three EBITDA turns. Analogous to the prior anecdote, only after the governance stabilized and clarity in disclosure improved, did analysts migrate the company into the leader group, and thus multiples converged upward.

1.4.3. The Cumulative Nature of Credibility

Credibility is built slowly and lost overnight. Companies that consistently meet or exceed guidance earn credibility, so when they miss, investors view it as an exception. Companies that overpromise create a credibility gap, and even when they deliver, investors view the results through a lens of disbelief.

A healthcare example illustrates the distinction. The company's equity value depended on clinical milestones, but management repeatedly set aggressive timelines that later slipped. Analysts began to treat delays as the base case and marked down their modeled valuations. When positive trial data finally arrived, the stock barely moved. Credibility had already been spent.

By contrast, a commodity-linked company showed discipline. Rather than forecasting prices it could not predict, it reported free cash flow sensitivity ranges against a consistent, agreed scenario each quarter. Investors rewarded that clarity and simplicity with a valuation premium. Trust established in one part of the disclosure framework can soften volatility elsewhere.

1.4.4. Behavioral Confirmation

The behavioral finance literature explains why building trust is a lengthy process. Anchoring ensures that investors view and interpret incoming data through prior credibility assessments. Confirmation bias solidifies existing beliefs. A company with a trusted credibility can "miss," and it is forgiven. A company without a trusted credibility can "miss" and be punished. The company with trusted credibility must take multiple consistent, disciplined disclosure steps before investors will accept a character model on the upside.

1.4.5. Process for Building Trust

Advisory practice contends that building trust does more than require better performance; it requires major design improvements in the disclosure framework. Metrics must be well-defined, need to be disclosed consistently over time, and need to be reconciled transparently. Investor perception must be systematically measured, never anecdotal, to track credibility gaps and dialogue.

Trust is built through repetition. You cannot replace it with a louder message.

1.5. Liquidity as Confidence

1.5.1. Liquidity is more than mechanics

Liquidity is often considered a maker, and index adder, and index adder, and index adder, to it. When liquidity disappears, it is usually due to an issue with disclosure. Investors trade freely in companies where they believe the information risk is low. They become illiquid when there is inconsistent disclosure.

1.5.2. When liquidity disappears

Consider a stable consumer company with solid fundamentals that nevertheless experienced volatile trading around earnings. At critical moments, irrational liquidity eroded. The cause was inconsistent disclosure. Analysts could no longer model the business with confidence, and investors preferred to avoid exposure when surprises were most likely.

Over the next three years, management developed discipline. They reported on the same operational drivers with consistent definitions each quarter. As a result, the estimated dispersion narrowed, liquidity improved, volatility declined, and ultimately, valuation rose. This happened not because the fundamentals improved, but because investors had enough confidence in the information to trade on it consistently.

1.5.3. Sovereign example

The sovereign debt market has similar behavior. An African country with mean fiscal metrics compared to peers had wider spreads and poor auction coverage. Investors pointed to the opacity. After quarterly fiscal briefings with sensitivity analysis, spreads were tightened by 20bps in six months. Liquidity came back after credibility.

1.5.4. Liquidity as a cost of capital driver

Liquidity is more than a convenience. It has an immediate and permanent impact on the cost of capital. Illiquid liquidity increases volatility and increases the cost of diluting institutional holders. The risk penalty for illiquidity is paid by others trying to invest: a higher implied discount rate and a smaller pool of investors willing to invest. The penalty is one of reputation, not structure.

1.5.5. Advisor method on liquidity

Advisors can diagnose market credibility with the spread curve and how the departure warning signs: liquidity lost credibility due to a reasonably wide pool of investor participation. The remedy to this situation is rarely a buyback program or other structural gimmicks. Essentially, it is consistent disclosure that convinces large pools of investors that risks are contained and shocks are minimized.

1.6. The listening curve and its transient properties

Attention, trust, and liquidity are in line. Engagement leads to credibility. Credibility leads to confidence. Confidence leads to liquidity. Liquidity leads to premium valuations. This is called the listening curve.

The listening curve is perilous. Companies navigate slowly to disciplined disclosure. Companies erase all efforts in the blink of an eye when the discipline is broken with a single breach. Exceedingly aggressive guidance is the most common breach. Not all investors just punish the miss with traders' price reaction, but price decreases for a certain amount of time. Time plus credibility is required to recover between the converging curves.

The implication is straightforward but significant: disclosure is not communicative; it is capital. Companies that recognized this preserved valuation stability in tumultuous markets. Companies that disregarded it structurally impaired their valuation.

1.7. Implications for companies and advisors

Markets do not listen equally. They listen selectively, allocating scarce attention to the companies that matter. Where trust was strong, valuations were held. Where it was weak, they compressed. Liquidity was present only when trust was prevalent. For advisors and executives, the penultimate question is not what disclosure you send, but why investors will listen, why they will trust, and why they will provide liquidity. Only then does disclosure become valuation.

Chapter 2.
Valuations Is All About Reputation

Valuation is often characterized by arithmetic: discounted cash flows, multiples, and comparison tables. Outputs look very precise, down to the decimal and sensitivities. But anyone who's been in the room with an analyst or banker while those models are constructed knows that arithmetic is anything but neutral. There's judgment embedded, and that judgment is based on reputation.

Reputation doesn't appear in a line item. It's rarely named. But it lives inside company-specific risk premiums, in the choice of peers, in assumptions of terminal growth, and in willingness to buy or discount guidance. In this way, valuation becomes less a top-decimal question and more a matter of what numbers the market will ascribe to the company.

2. Reputation Inside the Math

2.1. The Risk Premium in DCF

Discounted cash flow models are the basis of the cost of capital. Typically, analysts start with a market-wide equity risk premium and then adjust for company specifics. That adjustment is where credibility gets priced. Suppose the subject is a biotechnology company working through clinical trials. Then, for a management team with a conservative reputation, it could be modeled at 7-8 percent cost of equity versus a team that has consistently missed timelines (with a credibility penalty) at 10-12 percent. The mere two to four percentage point spread is a multiple (i.e., double digit) in potential net present value.

What's the delta? It's not a science risk. It's disclosure risk, or credibility risk. The analyst knows that if management follows through on timelines, then it requires less uncertainty. When management fails to hit or cuts down numbers, it will be plugged into the discount rate, just as leverage will be plugged into the discount rate. Terminal Growth Assumptions: The Terminal value is just to determine how much faith the company can maintain growth after the explicit forecast. An investable water trust team can probably pull 2% and maybe 3% terminal growth. An uninvestable water trust team can have 1% growth or a flat line. Over a 10-year model, the coequity of enterprise value.

Terminal groan endorsement of presumed durability. Credible management implies that reinvestment to grow will be deployable, expansion effort will continue, and the expansion will continue. Incredible management implies that reinvestment to grow will be destructive of value and will reduce assumptions linearly.

Peer Set Politics Comps as Judgement, Not Science. Relative valuation seems mechanically easy: choose your peer, apply your multiples, derive your implied value. Comps sheets are political. Which companies are included is a judgment. Analysts and investors use judgment not based only on size and industry, but also on management and credibility. An industry in Europe is a case in point. It had superior earnings growth compared to all peers, yet in every analyst's report, it was in the lowest peer grouping. The analysts said it was not worthy due to the continuous turnover of management and inconsistent reporting as a reason to move out of the superior peer grouping. The multiple gap of two to three EBITDA turns is not indicative of fundamentals, since the company had equally high-quality earnings. It is indicative of a reputation that unraveled. Only when governance reforms are in place, and the firm delivers stable reporting for two years, will it graduate into the leaders group.

2.2. How Bankers Create Peers

For IPOs, bankers often create "aspirational" peer groups to defend a premium. Investors will check these names carefully. For those firms where governance or disclosure does not justify the firm being there, investors will push back, and the bankers lose credibility. The advisor has to try to guess which peers the market will accept and not let reputation destroy the argument.

2.3. Premiums and Discounts by Sector

2.3.1. Energy and Capital Discipline

For energy, any reputation premiums are given to demonstrate capital discipline. If two firms have the same reserves and production levels, they can be valued at different multiples. A company that has a history of returning cash to investors and provides clear planning on capital upfront will get a higher valuation than a company with the opposite reputation, or one that mixes and matches multiple definitions.

2.3.2. Consumer Clarity

For consumers, clear tracking of unit economics earns a premium. Firms that consistently report traffic, ticket, mix, and margin development are seen as reliable. Firms that leave investors guessing, or that play with definitions of traffic, are discounted. If analysts cannot model your business, they will move you to the back of the line and apply a risk premium.

2.3.3. Financials and Risk Transparency

Banks show that reputational issues can bring down valuation. Two banks that are identical on the balance sheet are valued at different book multiples. The delta is mostly in transparent disclosure. Banks that clearly outline risk exposures, set out stress tests, tell you what the asset quality is, and provide consistent updates keep their reputational premium intact. Banks that obscure their risks, often in footnotes, get discounted even if their metrics look good.

2.3.4. Technology

In technology, execution is the basis for valuing stocks. Growth stocks that consistently and stably disclose their key user metrics, user churn, and user monetization opportunities can maintain relatively high valuation multiples. Growth stock companies that are inconsistent in the definitions of the metrics or inflate the metrics are "punished," even if they achieve growth. Investors price both the potential of an opportunity and the probability of achieving that potential.

2.4. Investor Psychology and the Stickiness of Reputation

2.4.1. Anchor All in Models

Once the market forms a credibility judgment, it tends to stick. A company with a long track record of overpromising will eventually see sell-side analysts and the buy side trim their projections, even after execution improves. Models start to handicap the story by shifting probability weight toward the base or downside case and by applying a lower valuation multiple. At that point, the reputational penalty is effectively locked in.

2.4.2. Confirmation Bias on the Note

Analysts look for evidence to confirm their view. Those who trust management teams will soften their wording, using phrases like "temporary headwinds" or "execution issues." Those who distrust management will be far more critical, using terms such as "structural weakness" or "non-sustainable beats." Their language shapes buy-side perception, reinforcing the idea that valuation spreads are widening for a reason.

2.4.3. Investment Committee

On the buy-side, allocation decisions are based on credibility judgments. At an investment committee meeting, debate over the stock centers not only on the numbers but also on trust in management. A management team with a dent in their credibility will be heavily scrutinized in full committee and receive a smaller allocation and reduced commitment. The opposite is also true: as management builds credibility over time, committees extend their patience and reward the stock with larger allocations and firmer commitments.

This kind of asymmetry is what explains why reputational redemption takes time and is complicated. One quarter of good results does not erase skepticism built over a three or four-year period, especially if the pre-report stock price valuations were earnings-based. Prior perceptions, positive or negative, typically require multiple periods of consistent proof before capital is reallocated back to levels that prevailed before the reputational penalty.

2.5. How to Measure the Reputation Gap

2.5.1. Estimate Dispersion

Simply measuring the degree of estimate dispersion would yield a quantitative measure of credibility in the management team. Dispersion is a signal of doubt in the management's story, whether the volatility is structural to the industry or related to credibility.

2.5.2. Perception Audits and Sentiment Coding

Perception audits take it a step further. By interviewing investors and therefore coding their language, advisors identify the reputational characteristics. Terms "disciplined" or "transparent" are associated with premiums. Terms "promotional" or "opaque" suggest a discount. Audit of sentiment over time gives an observable marker of trust and how to track reputational recovery or fall.

2.5.3. Hidden Haircuts in Analyst Models

Analysts are sometimes a source of hidden haircuts when they potentially discount forecasts for a company. For example, if a company provides guidance of $1.00 EPS, they could publish a forecast of $0.80. The haircut is more than aesthetic; it is the market's price for credibility risk. To locate hidden haircuts is simply a matter of identifying comparisons between management guidance, analyst forecasts, and understanding the differences that have occurred.

2.6. Closing Trust Gaps with Disclosure Architecture

2.6.1. Key Performance Indicators Architecture

Closing gaps of trust requires structural changes to disclosure, not a louder message about trust. Key performance must be selected with intent, defined with precision, and provided consistently.

For example, a technology company that was under the influence of credibility discounts underwrote its disclosures using very specific parameters; active users, churn, and monetization were explicitly defined, reconciled to the financials, and disclosed quarterly. After six quarters of consistent disclosure, the haircuts were stricken. Rather than the reported financials changing, multiples improved.

2.6.2. Proving Sufficiently Short

What does this mean? Repetition is ideal. Investors grant trust only after consistent, verifiable disclosure is established, and the process compounds over time. Early signals of renewed trust can look noisy, even random. Each cycle of delivery forces investors to retest their models. Recognition of improvement is earned through repetition, with less rhetoric and more consistent proof.

2.7. Trust in Sovereign Debt Markets

2.7.1. Spreads as Credibility Markup

Sovereign debt markets price institutional credibility. Two countries with similar debt-to-GDP ratios may still face materially different borrowing costs. The spread reflects the risk premium investors demand for weaker institutions and policy credibility.

2.7.2. Transparency and Rating Agencies

Credit rating agencies emphasize an environment of trust. Countries that provide consistent, transparent disclosure tend to sustain higher ratings and tighter spreads. By contrast, opaque reporting or political instability can trigger downgrades and widen spreads as investors demand a credibility premium.

2.7.3. Example as an illustration

An African government provides more examples of this. Despite watching fiscal ratios comparable to those of other African peers, receiving quotes from multiple sources provided wide spreads and generally weak coverage. Investor sentiment was a lack of transparency, or at least being upfront. A solution was to provide quarterly consolidated fiscal briefings and support sensitivity analysis. After approximately six months, spreads tightened around twenty basis points. The market price of trust helped reduce the capital cost directly.

2.7.4. Trust as Invisible Capital

In other words, trust is not listed on a balance sheet. But trust is capitalized upon every day by market participants. It is contained in risk spreads, peer spreads, multiples, and spreads. It persists in misestimations or stakes that trust. It is suggested through spreads, audits, and trimmed money. And repeated through the disclosure of product architecture.

For companies, pricing and value never shift solely based on numbers alone. It is a combination of numbers and trust. For advisors, the opportunity is to find trust discounts, establish closed loops to a closed loop to trusts, and establish conditions once re-established. In capital markets, trust means not to overpay for the cost of capital.

Chapter 3.
The Work of the Capital Markets Advisor

Companies frequently misunderstand investor relations. They reduce it to logistics: calls and scripts, investor days, and earnings releases. But logistics are only the tip of the iceberg. Below the surface, there is strategy. The purpose of the capital markets advisor is to build and maintain credibility in a way that can be measured in valuation, cost of capital, and access to liquidity.

The advisor isn't writing the scripts for the externalization of operations. The advisor is a strategist who operates at the intersection of finance, communications, and governance. The work of the advisor is to interpret operational states into market logic, to maintain and build credibility amidst challenges, to integrate across silos, and to protect boundaries that ensure trust. This chapter explores each of these facets, considering how reputation accrues to valuation through disciplined advisory work.

3. Interpreting: Converting Operations into Market Logic

3.1. Why Interpreting Is Important

Executives think and talk in terms of operations. Finance thinks and talks in terms of valuation. If there is no interpretation, communication fails.

An example of this could be the redesign of a supply chain, which might be discussed internally in terms of throughput and scrap. The external conversation needs to be about margin stability and free cash flow security. Or, a new product line might be discussed internally in terms of innovation and design. The investor needs to know if it grows addressable markets, reduces concentration risk, and affirms terminal growth assumptions.

Interpreting is not simplification. It is the work of taking the mechanics of a business and translating them into variables that an investor can model.

3.2. Method of Interpreting

The advisors create what we might call "interpreting tables." The interpreting tables are associated internally with external measures of valuation. For example:

- Throughput → Increase in Gross Margin
- Decrease scrap → Predictable cash flow
- Productivity of unit → SG&A efficiency
- Customer churn → Assumptions for cost of capital.

This type of translation requires knowledge of the particulars of operations and languages of finance. It is a two-way street: absorbing stories from managers and engineers to expressing the source of value in a financial language that they understand and are willing to pay for.

3.2.1. A Case Example

One global insurer presented a major accounting adjustment as technical housekeeping. Investors labeled it as noise. Some advisory work repackaged that accounting treatment as evidence of capital efficiency and highlighted how the new accounting policy released surplus capital and mitigated reinvestment risk. Investors saw the same "fact", but instead of focusing on accounting boundaries, they focused on financial valuation, and the perspective in the market shifted. Translation alleviated confusion and invoked belief.

3.3. Establishing Belief and in Reactive Situations

3.3.1. Activist Campaigns

Activists establish information asymmetry. They articulate compelling stories that are simple, as they build on selective parts of management disclosure. Charting a peer outperformance performance, selection scenarios of transaction pricing, and returns of capital to shareholders have a greater impact than laborious management slides on the incoherence of performance.

Across an advisor, management flack gets cut off at the knees, and the attention focuses on:

- Deconstructing activist story and positioning on management disclosure.
- Road-testing of activist claims against scenarios.
- Mapping boundaries where management disclosure impacts investors.
- Generating a counter-descriptive story along those boundaries.

Consider a mid-cap manufacturer facing pressure from slowing growth. The simplest activist story gained traction because management's disclosures provided no clarity on margin improvement. Once disclosures were adjusted to clearly explain cost per unit, utilization, and allocation, tracking became possible. Weaknesses were disclosed openly, and strengths were justified with numbers. Management won over investors, and a settlement preserved the strategy with only limited governance changes.

The takeaway: activists do not win just because they are right. Activists win when they have more credibility than management. Advisors render the credibility playing field even.

3.3.2. Litigation and Crisis

Litigation and crisis events will test credibility even more harshly. Counsel would recommend silence, as they are liable and presumably want to avoid liability. The market interprets silence as covering up. In the absence of a voice, investors assume the worst-case scenario will play out.

In a particular case, a company with a regulatory inquiry exposed the outline of their potential exposures and the internal controls preventing them. This allowed investors to hedge downside risk. The stock dropped on disclosure, but less than it had dropped on the rumor. Liquidity remained orderly. Uncertainty fell, and credibility held.

The advisory approach in a crisis is calibration: disclose enough to allow investors to model risk responsibly, while staying within the boundaries of the law. Not enough disclosure severs credibility; too much disclosure creates liability. Advisors maintain the pressure.

3.4. Integration Between Silos

3.4.1. Why Integration Matters

Finance, strategy, and communications often operate in silos. Finance provides the numbers, strategy provides the perspective, and communication supplies the words. When they are not aligned, the seams show, and investors perceive them as risks.

Advisors integrate the silos. They ensure that strategy connects to financial disclosure, communications connect to actual numbers, and offer guidance that finance captures the insights investors need. Integrating establishes credibility because the investor can put all of the inputs together into a single "story."

3.4.2. Method of Integration

Integration depends on having a process in place. Advisors, at times, create "disclosure councils" that synchronize finance, strategy, and communications before they report externally. They make templates that align operational KPIs with financial KPI. They even coach management to create consistent definitions regardless of context.

A sovereign is a classic case. Fiscal authorities, central banks, and line ministries often issue uncoordinated statements. The result is chaos. An advisory process aligned the messaging, established quarterly briefings, and integrated fiscal and monetary data into a single disclosure frame. Markets responded with tighter spreads and deeper liquidity.

3.5. Setting Boundaries

3.5.1. Guarding Against Overpromising

The number one killer of credibility is overpromising. Eager guidance may ease the immediate pain, but one miss can erase years of credibility. Advisors help by setting boundaries and promoting guidance ranges that management can stand behind, even under stress.

A technology company considering an IPO wanted to forecast mild profitability within two years. Advisors stress-tested the assumptions and showed management that the outcome was achievable only in a best-case scenario. The guidance was rescheduled and reframed as a range with specific parameters. When actual results fell within that range, the markets rewarded the company with renewed credibility.

3.5.2. Ethics as Strategy

Managing ethical boundaries is a type of boundary management seen in some companies. Some think they can fool everyone through selective disclosure, descriptors loaded with exaggeration, and the press. They may get a short-term advantage, but destroy long-term confidence. Markets, too, have a long memory. Advisors accepting this type of behavior not only degrade their own reputation, but also the cost of capital. The value is that it is the advisor's credibility. Credibility must be protected.

3.6. IPOs as a Validation of Advisory Process

3.6.1. Teaching the Model

An IPO is a sandbox for advisory work. Bankers may highlight aspirational peer groups and a growing top line. Investors think a bit more in-depth on unit economics, disciplined reinvestment, and governance.

One growth company initially stated in its prospectus that it was focused on top-line growth. Investors were wary. Advisors worked on the structure of the disclosures around their acquisition cost, churn rate, and monetization, which was aligned with the financial statement. They were also able to demonstrate the IPO model in their roadshow presentations on the elements that investors could model. The IPO was successful, and aftermarket volatility was less than that of its peer group.

The advisory principle is rather simple; IPOs work when you teach the market how to model the business. If you do not teach the market, capital will give you a discount. If you teach the market, they will score above the line and evaluate.

3.6.2. Measuring Success in the Advisory Process

Advisors must evaluate success through market results, not slick materials. The measures are:

- Smaller dispersion of estimates.
- Lower volatility around disclosures.
- Longer-term ownership.
- Tighter spreads and better liquidity.
- Ability to raise capital in poor markets, on good terms.

When these happen, credibility has been preserved, and valuation protected. When these don't occur, it does not matter how good the materials look; this advisory process is a failure.

3.6.3. Credibility and the Advisor Strategy

The capital markets advisor is not the investor communications officer. The advisor is the strategy for converting credibility into valuation. The advisor teaches how to convert operations into investor logic, defends it under duress, integrates across silos of the advisory team, and holds the boundaries true. In doing this, the advisor gives valuation sustainability and trust in management.

Management that treats its investor relations as surface messaging does not understand the stakes. Those who see their investor relations as a strategy get that capital is a disclosure, trust is currency, and credibility is the most meaningful asset to hold.

Part II.
The Playbook

Chapter 4.
Crafting the Equity Story

The term equity story permeates discussions about the public markets, yet it is seldom defined in a manner that adequately satisfies the precision investors seek. In pitch books, it becomes a cocktail of adjectives. In roadshows, it becomes a slide on the total addressable market. In quarterly materials, it morphs into leadership or customer obsession. None of these options carries a value premium. Markets do not pay for words. They pay for information they can model.

An equity story is not a catchy phrase. An equity story is an architecture of confidence. It is the architecture for showing investors how you build cash flow, how that cash flow is protected by risks, and how capital is directed to develop value. When the architecture is present and is done with discipline, value becomes steady, the company-specific risk premium diminishes, and long-horizon owners build. When the architecture is absent or incoherent, forecasts differ, liquidity disappears when needed, and valuations drop when the fundamentals of the business appear strong.

The aim of this chapter is to make the equity story tangible. The equity story requires converting a strategy to modelable variables, validating those variables through disclosures, calibrating aspirations to what the market will believe, using the company lifecycles and investor perspective to inform the sequencing of the narrative, and enforcing a rhythm that provides investors the opportunity to detect the pattern. The financial theories lay out the rationale for why this works. The signaling theory outlines the framework of signaling, and the costly agency theory describes why investors use governance and disclosures in a discount rate.

Narrativenomic and behavioral finance reveal how narratives resolve uncertainty and how sticky credibility is modeled.

4.1. The equity story as a model

Narrative and story are not synonymous. Narrative is exposition. Story is architecture. Investors cannot capitalize nouns. They can only capitalize verbs. Therefore, the equity story must be articulated in the same language of capitalization: what drives revenue & gross profit, what stabilizes operating leverage, what leads to cash generation from earnings, and how reinvestment and distribution choices change the angle of long-term value creation.

Take, for example, a universal bank that labels itself a digital innovator. That label has no modeling content. Now, suppose the same bank articulated that adoption of digital capabilities reduced branch interactions per customer by a given percentage, that it decreased cost to income by a given measure, those dollars were repurposed towards risk analytics that reduced credit losses, and the cumulative effect bolstered sustained return on equity in the long run. In the second scenario, there are variables and causative relationships that an investor can input into a model. That is what equity stories must do.

Failure to is predictable. Excess theory creates noise because investors cannot derive what is relevant. Promotional drift reduces credibility because guidance movements are necessarily neglected and miss the pile on. Missequencing is disruptive because early-stage companies insist on framing long-term vision when investors seek evidence of economics, and mature companies use growth language when investors prefer determination of capital return. All operational impediments are embedded in discount rates and peer selection, so they show up as spread and multiple, other than commentary.

4.2 Identifying the true drivers of variance

The first half is diagnostic. Which operational inputs drive variance in free cash flow over time? We start with stats. We end with the manager's judgment. A statistically corroborated approach will require running each quarter's candidates one by one against free cash flow and operating profit, along with sensitivity to reasonable shocks. The output will be very few candidates, which drives most of the variability.

For retail, typically, it will be traffic, average ticket, gross margin, and working capital cadence, being a second-order impact. For subscription software, it is typically active users, churn, or net revenue retention, and monetization per user; acquisition payback is a control. For regulated utilities, it is typically rate base growth, allowed return, and cost control. These drivers will cover all industries, which is why investors are not memorizing every internal KPI. They are conflicted with trying to identify which few drive the cash flow story.

Once we have identified the drivers, we must tell the story around the drivers. This is not the same as throwing out everything else. This is maximizing the dominant drivers and having other things support the dominant drivers. Consistency in terms! When a company alters a KPI definition without a bridge, the learning curve starts over, and management is instead optimizing optics, not teaching the market how to model.

One retailer that used to publish more than thirty operating metrics provides an illustrative example. The analysts were arguing about what was moving cash. Everything was all over the place, and the stock was trading below peers even though the store economics were similar. The disciplined redesign focused on traffic, basket size, and margin at the center. They fit each one to the financial statements and reconciled against GAAP revenue and EBIT on the same page. Over six quarters, the spread in forecasted earnings fell apart quickly, liquidity around earnings improved, and the multiple spread shrank. The stores never changed. Just the learning system.

4.3. Proof vs. promise

Investors have a persistent bias toward proof over narrative. A company that leads with ambition but does not supply interim proof points creates narrative overhang. That overhang gets priced as risk, raising the company-specific risk premium in the cost of equity, compressing sell-side models, and shortening holding periods on the buy side.

The antidote is disclosure architecture. The phrase has three components. First, the metrics that carry the story are defined and calculated the same way every period. Second, those metrics are reconciled to the financial statements in a way that allows an analyst to build a bridge without guesswork. Third, major initiatives are tied to auditable milestones that management commits to report on, whether they are met or slip. The burden of proof shifts from adjectives to cadence.

This architecture is costly. Costly architecture requires stable definitions and a willingness to report misses in public. That cost is what gives the framework signaling value. Cheap signals do not separate credibility from noise. Costly signals, repeated, do.

A renewable developer provides a textbook case. For a time, it sold optimism on capacity additions and revenue growth. The Street applied a haircut to every forecast because execution and project finance risk were not visible in public disclosure. The company then changed the mechanism. It disclosed executed offtake agreements by counterparty, disclosed capex commitments and construction milestones, and reconciled expected megawatts to expected EBITDA milestone by milestone. As projects were delivered, the haircut narrowed and the multiple expanded, without any change in the core equipment. The market paid for proof of process, not just the outcome.

4.4. Calibrating ambition to credibility

Ambition is not the enemy. Uncalibrated ambition is. Each company has a line of credibility. The payoff curve expresses the potential claims the market is willing to entertain based on the team's credibility and the nature of business risk. The payoff curve can be moved outward by consistently delivering within a defined range, taking misses without excuse, and maintaining stable definitions. It snaps back when management signals above its earned range.

Calibrating ambition starts with a cold look at what can be accomplished without 100% execution. It occasionally means publishing a Lower bound that is conservative inside the company but reasonable when thinking about realistic supply, hiring, demand, or regulatory timing constraints. It also means clarifying what will happen if the timing is worse than expected. This is not meant to kill energy. The intent is to prevent a miss that would reset the company's credibility for a number of periods.

Some companies attempt to stand out from their peers. In industrials, there are cherished companies that act like industry disruptors, without the economics, and they are punished with interest. You're not only barred by peers that you hope to join, but also by the peers that you should be compared to. A better approach is to earn progression by accessing capital discipline and margin improvement that (mean) justify progress out of peers with similar growth rates and just let buy-side move the comp table.

4.5. Sequencing the equity story

The equity story develops based on the corporate stage. Early on, investors need unit economics and proof that the product or service has a real need. At scale, this can provide operational efficiency, competitive advantage, and improved predictability of cash flow. At maturity, it becomes a capital return discipline and strength through challenges. It is confusing to tell a late-stage story at an early stage. Early-stage stories at a late stage frustrate.

Sequencing also shows up around events. Investors need to see, early, the metrics they will be using post IPO. When a company plans to disclose those metrics later, it raises alarm bells. In a turnaround, investors are looking for a handful of operating controls that can deliver the first two quarters of repair, and how those controls map to a twelve-month and twenty-month horizon. In an expansion into foreign markets, investors need a capital allocation framework by geography, controls for political and currency risk, and clear rules for when to pause, exit, or reverse course if circumstances change.

The advisor's responsibility is to frame the story so it fits the stage, the event, and the audience. This is not tone painting. It is an oversight of how the company intends to be perceived and funded.

4.6. Global climate and investor priorities

Investor priorities are not the same across regions. In developed markets, capital return discipline, transparent risk governance, and environmental disclosure are often the most important factors. In emerging markets, governance, policy stability, and hard currency reserves are involved. A sovereign or corporate entity that addresses the wrong priorities will appear to be tone deaf, even if its numbers are correct. This does not call for a different story to be told in every market; it provides focus on the pieces of the story that the target base cares about and supports that focus with measurable commitments. The sequence applies to sovereigns, quasi-sovereigns, and corporates. Credibility is ultimately a function of what is disclosed, how it is assured, and if it sustains through political and commodity cycles.

4.7. A systematic playbook for construction

A complete playbook can be articulated in separation as a genre that runs continuously instead of an event in marketing. Start with an audit to determine which operating variables account for the majority of the variance in cash generation over time. Build your architecture of disclosure around those variables with definitions that are fixed and bridges from those variables to the financial statements. Anchor ambition to the actual credibility curve, not the curve that management wishes existed. Publish ranges that can be delivered without perfect runs. Sequence the narrative to the stage of the company and the event you are addressing and surface the investor priorities that truly motivate allocation in that audience. Iterate through the reporting periods until the Street's models converge and the language used in coverage illustrates faith in discipline, rather than improvisation. When the language and the dispersion reflect learning, consider expanding ambition a notch and repeat the sequence.

The rest of this chapter demonstrates the method in practice with three public cases. They are selected because the underlying facts are publicly observable and, together, they represent a full credibility life cycle: launch, regain, and sovereign credibility. The cases that follow are based on publicly available company disclosures, market data, and contemporaneous media reporting, and are presented for educational and illustrative purposes.

4.7.1. Case 1: Tech at launch, Snowflake in 2020

Setting: The software IPO cohort of 2019 and 2020 came to market under the cloud of rocky or failed launches. Investors were increasingly skeptical of Total Addressable Market claims, had moderated their priors toward evidence of monetization or retention, and wanted to know whether revenue growth was driven by uneconomic acquisition or whether cohorts expanded without disproportionate cost. Skepticism surrounded churn, the sustainability of consumption models, and the bridge from operating losses to positive cash flow.

Disclosure gap: Many issuers over-indexed on total addressable market and customer logos while underdelivering the operating metrics investors need to model sustainability. Without credible disclosure on net revenue retention, cohort behavior, and payback, the market often relied on indirect inference and applied a credibility discount to forward growth assumptions.

Case analysis: Snowflake's S-1 and roadshow materials emphasized evidence over adjectives. The company highlighted net revenue retention in excess of 160 percent and supported it with cohort-based disclosure that illustrated expansion within existing customers. It connected the dynamics of a consumption model to GAAP performance with clear bridges and framed gross margin trajectory with operational explanation rather than timing promises. The disclosures provided enough granularity to evaluate whether growth was being purchased through economics that would later revert or earned through durable cohort expansion.

Result: These revealed metrics served as anchors for underwriting. Sell-side models and buy-side debate centered on net revenue retention and cohort expansion as the basis for forward growth rather than on market sizing slides. The offering was priced above the initial range, and the aftermarket discussion concentrated on the drivers the company had taught the market to track. Relative to peers that did not provide comparable proof points, post IPO volatility appeared more orderly. The lesson is not that a single metric drove valuation. The lesson is that an equity story at launch works when it teaches the market which variables matter, and then attaches those variables to financial statements through definitions that do not drift.

4.7.2. Case two: rebuilding consumer credibility, Chipotle, 2015 to 2019

Context: A health and safety crisis tarnished Chipotle's reputation in 2015. Traffic declined, media scrutiny persisted, and investors were left uncertain about the durability of a recovery. Estimates diverged materially, and the stock's multiple compressed. Trading volatility around earnings also increased, consistent with a market that lacked a stable framework for measuring whether recovery signals were structural or transient.

Disclosure gap: The company disclosed a number of operational items, but the market did not converge on a small set of variables that could serve as the primary recovery scorecard. Analysts debated which indicators reflected genuine demand normalization versus short-lived promotional activity. The buy side responded by haircutting guidance, trimming forward assumptions, and shortening holding periods until a more dependable control loop could be observed.

Management response: Management reoriented disclosure around a limited set of drivers tied directly to cash flow generation. Same-store sales, average check, and restaurant-level margin became central. Digital order penetration and loyalty adoption were positioned as drivers that could be interpreted through traffic, mix, and unit economics rather than treated as marketing highlights. Over time, the company reinforced definitions consistently and linked operating indicators back to GAAP revenue and operating performance through repeatable bridges. Qualitative commentary emphasized the operational processes through which variables could move rather than asserting timetable promises.

Outcome: Through a methodical, quarter-by-quarter cadence over an extended period, the estimate dispersion narrowed and the coverage posture shifted from skepticism to cautious support to growing confidence that the control loop was functioning. The multiple recovered materially from crisis-era levels and, over time, moved toward a premium relative to casual dining peers. The central message is not that Chipotle returned to growth. It is that the market rewarded a credible recovery process because the disclosure system taught investors how to model recovery, and it continued teaching without drift until the framework became routine.

4.7.3. Case three: Sovereign credibility via disclosure, Mexico sovereign green bond, 2019

Context: Sovereign debt pricing can diverge meaningfully from simple ratio math, even when headline macro metrics appear comparable, because institutional credibility influences the risk premium investors require. In 2019, Mexico sought to diversify its investor base and reduce its cost of capital in a politically volatile environment while signaling improved macro discipline prospectively. ESG-oriented investors were already skeptical of greenwashing and wanted a framework that could be substantiated over time rather than a one-time label.

Disclosure gap: Traditional fiscal disclosure systems address public finance fundamentals but do not, on their own, establish the governance and traceability ESG investors require for labeled proceeds. Investors lacked a credible mechanism to validate that proceeds would be allocated as committed and that impact would be tracked consistently. Without that confidence, ESG-dedicated capital was less likely to engage meaningfully, and pricing benefits associated with incremental demand were less likely to be realized.

Disclosure shift: Mexico developed a Sustainable Finance Framework that specified eligible project categories aligned to UN Sustainable Development Goals, governance around project selection, treatment of proceeds allocation and tracking, and a commitment to periodic allocation and impact reporting subject to external review. The framework did not rely on adjectives. It established a repeatable disclosure system that stakeholders could assess at issuance and then revisit through ongoing reporting.

Outcome: Order books were reportedly strong, participation broadened, and secondary performance and spread behavior improved relative to what would have been expected absent incremental demand and greater confidence in proceeds governance. Continuous reporting helped sustain the framework and made the label durable rather than episodic. The point is not that legal form, ratings, or macro fundamentals were transformed by the instrument. The point is that a credible disclosure system, aligned with investor priorities and reinforced through repeatable reporting, can lower the cost of capital by expanding the buyer set and strengthening trust in the use of proceeds.

4.8. Closing: teaching the market to model

An equity story works when it allows investors to build a model they believe in and then rewards that belief with delivery inside stable definitions. The practice is not cosmetic. It is a system. Identify the few variables that explain most of the variance in cash. Build disclosure around them with reconciliations that do not drift. Set ambition inside the range you can deliver, then expand the range by delivering. Sequence the story to stage and to the event at hand, and emphasize the priorities that the actual buyers care about.

Repeat until the Street's models converge and until language moves from hope to proof.

When companies do this, the market prices discipline rather than adjectives. The company-specific risk premium falls, ownership lengthens, liquidity becomes more reliable in stress, and capital can be raised on fair terms. When companies do not do this, no volume of promotion can prevent discounts from forming. The equity story is not decoration. It is the method by which belief is converted into valuation.

Chapter 5. Covering Analysts and Targeting Investors

5.1. The Importance of Analysts and Targeting Investors

Coverage and targeting are often reduced to numbers. Companies crow about how many analysts are covering them, or how many investors they met with on their roadshow. Investor relations teams log where they traveled to conferences, and provide reports indicating their activities. And while none of these ways is what really counts.

Coverage and targeting are not administrative; they are architectural. They shape, ultimately, how the company is known, its stature, and the extent of the ongoing story, and investors are allocated capital based on how they have their mandates. They do not just buy or sell - investors approve or disapprove the story based on their style, held positions, constraints, and horizon.

When strategically designed coverage and targeting are used, credibility stacks. Analysts hold up the correct architecture, and investors fund it with conviction. When they are left alone, credibility fragments. Analysts focused their attention on surface variables that are only moments. Marginal pricing is determined by investors with short-horizon mandates. Valuation is fragile.

This chapter describes how analysts are translators of credibility, how coverage can fail or succeed as a result of whether it is cultivated, and how investors represent not a crowd, but constituencies with mandates. It illustrates how architecture can be both built and destroyed, across multiple sectors, through cases.

5.2. Analysts as Guardians of Credibility

5.2.1. Role of Analysts

Analysts are held privileged with a level of access to information. They are able to engage management with direct phone calls during earnings calls and meetings on a one-on-one basis. They can publish models that define consensus. They write research notes that are shared across the buy side and are frequently the first filters applied by generalist portfolio managers to interpret a company's business.

In theory, analysts mediate asymmetric information. They are able to distil unprocessed disclosures into structured output. In practice, they make decisions. They select which operating metrics to incorporate into the model and those that are omitted. They decide to prioritize revenue growth, profit margin discipline, and cash conversion. They determine which peer sets and characterize multiples. They create the language that, through repetition, summarizes the process in value conversations.

Thus, they are not neutral players. Some are bound to banking relationships and are compensated for representing optimism. Some have reputations built on rigor and skepticism, and their notes are impactful with long-only funds. Advisors who understand the political economy recognize that analysts should be educated, not assumed to process properly.

5.2.2. Educating Analysts in a Systematic Way

Just offering the disclosure is not adequate. Analysts need to allow them to learn to model the company correctly. This will take more than merely giving analysts Onboarding materials. It requires going through the analysis with detailed explanations, each step, and the reason why they matter, how it reconciles to GAAP, and how others do not.

The discipline kicks off with a consensus mapping. Advisors will compare analyst models line by line and document where the differentiation occurs.

They pinpoint which assumptions affect the variance of estimates. They then focus education on these levers. For example, if some analysts reason volume growth creates revenue while others cite pricing, advisors must explain why one is more important and reconcile it to reported revenue.

This teaching must be consistent across cycles. Analysts do not adopt a framework after a single conversation. They need to see the variables repeated, reconciled, and demonstrated as obtainable over multiple quarters. Success is evident when coverage notes begin to use management's framing, peer sets are updated, and estimate dispersion narrows. At that point, analysts are no longer simply publishing data. They are reinforcing the credibility structure.

5.2.2.1. Case: Microsoft and Cloud Shift

Microsoft's progression toward the cloud in the early 2010s illustrates how disciplined investor education can reframe an entire company. At the time, the market largely treated Microsoft as a mature incumbent. Coverage often centered on PC shipments and Windows license revenue, and valuation multiples reflected a belief that the core business faced secular pressure.

Operational change alone was not enough. Investor relations and management began to teach the market a different set of variables. Through repeated briefings and consistent disclosure, analysts were walked through recurring revenue mechanics, customer economics, scale, and margin potential. The company provided investors with a clearer bridge between recurring revenue indicators and GAAP reporting so that the migration could be underwritten rather than assumed.

Over time, analyst models and narratives adjusted. Reports placed greater emphasis on cloud traction, recurring revenue dynamics, and capital allocation discipline. Peer comparisons also shifted. Microsoft was increasingly analyzed alongside platform and software peers with recurring economics rather than as a slow-growth legacy incumbent. The re-rating did not happen by accident. It happened when the variables were taught, repeated, and then validated through results that could be modeled consistently.

5.2.2.2. Case Study: WeWork's Coverage Failure

WeWork's failed IPO process in 2019 is a case study in what happens when narrative runs ahead of underwriteable economics. In the period leading up to the attempted offering, public discussion often leaned on broad themes such as disruption and community. However, the elements investors needed to underwrite a durable public equity story were not presented in a way that could withstand scrutiny. Unit economics, cash flow trajectory, and governance became central questions, and credible answers were required.

Once the S-1 was filed and the offering entered a more formal evaluation phase, investors began to assess the business model, governance structure, and path to sustainable economics with greater rigor. Without a consistent analytical framework that investors could reconcile to financial statements and operating drivers, confidence deteriorated quickly. Valuation expectations reset sharply relative to prior private market marks, and the transaction did not proceed.

Lesson: Coverage that repeats themes without enforceable variables is fragile. What holds is not positivity, but proof. A company that asks the market to trust a story must do the work of teaching investors how to model it, and then must keep that teaching consistent until the model can survive skepticism.

5.3. Investors a.k.a. Stakeholders

5.3.1. Mandates Reflect Activity

Just as analysts are not interchangeable, investors are not interchangeable. Quality of ownership can matter as much as quality of earnings because mandates differ in style, holding period, risk tolerance, and constraints. Hedge funds can provide liquidity and accelerate price discovery, but they can also increase volatility. Passive funds invest mechanically and cannot be avoided. Concentrated long-only ownership can provide stability and upside if those owners are aligned with the drivers of the equity story.

The question, as always, is who the marginal buyer is. In volatility, the marginal buyer becomes price sensitive. When the marginal buyer is aligned with what actually drives value, the valuation framework holds. When the marginal buyer is misaligned, volatility becomes the mechanism of discovery.

5.3.2. Case Study: Tesla's early volatility

In the early 2010s, Tesla's shareholder base included a large component of retail enthusiasm and momentum-oriented capital. Volatility was extreme. Earnings and news flow produced large price swings, and valuation multiples compressed quickly when sentiment weakened. The marginal buyer was often misaligned with the long-duration nature of a transformation story.

Greater stability began to emerge as Tesla produced clearer evidence of scale, improving margins, and repeatable execution. Long only institutions with longer horizons and higher tolerance for interim volatility began to take meaningful positions. As holding periods lengthened, the shareholder base became more resilient, valuation stabilized, and the implied cost of capital fell.

Tesla illustrates both extremes of targeting. Misaligned ownership creates fragility. Aligned ownership compounds credibility. The difference is not only operational. It depends on who is underwriting the operating path.

5.3.3. Case Study: Chipotle recovery

In 2015, Chipotle's food safety crisis impaired credibility. Analysts disagreed on which variables mattered most, estimate dispersion widened, investor time horizons shortened, and valuation multiples contracted.

Management responded by narrowing the external scorecard to a small set of operating variables tied to cash flow generation, including same-store sales, average check, and restaurant-level margins. Over time, consistent disclosure and repeatable definitions helped drive greater modeling convergence.

Ownership dynamics also mattered. As the recovery thesis became more legible, long-only investors with mandates suited to underwriting multi-quarter repair increasingly participated. As their stakes grew, turnover tended to decline, volatility moderated, and valuation recovered. The recovery was not purely operational. It was also architectural. Analysts aligned on the right drivers, investors with aligned mandates funded the pathway, and credibility was rebuilt across both the story and the shareholder base.

5.4. Coverage and Targeting are Architecture

Coverage and targeting must be architecture. It must not be left up to fate. Analysts must have the right variables before them, show them how to connect those variables, and engage them until use is visible. Investors must be segmented by mandate and targeted on purpose. Success is not based on how many activities, but if the consensus condenses, the language coalesces, and the shareholder base conforms.

The role of the advisor is that of an architect. This work entails delving into analyst models to see where misalignments lie, employing perception studies to explore trust issues around disclosure, mapping the shareholder mandates to discover who dictates marginal price, and repeatedly updating disclosures and targeting until constituency is reinforcing credibility.

It is a process. It doesn't happen in one or two quarters. Analysts adopt frameworks over a span of time. Investors take a stance on holding periods. The architecture builds gradually, and once constructed, maintains value throughout cycles.

5.5. Constituency is Architecture

The equity story cannot exist in a vacuum. It must be translated by analysts and funded by investors. The analysts dictate what variables create consensus. The investors dictate whether the consensus variables warrant capital. Collectively, they create credibility.

Companies that have coverage and targeting design embedded in their consistency have durability, lower cost of capital, and increased multiples. They educated analysts purposefully. They targeted mandates thoughtfully. They measured consensus and edited purposefully. Companies that neglect these dimensions can operationally perform well but still receive discounted prices, perplexed by how fundamentals do not justify returns.

In capital markets, valuation is not viewed in isolation. Valuation is viewed through constituencies. To manage valuation, a company must manage the architecture of constituencies. Analysts and investors are not spectators. They are the system.

Chapter 6. Earnings as an Operating System

Earnings represent the most explicit moment in the life of a public company. Once every ninety days, the market comes together to check if management can produce results, exemplify discipline, and justify the valuation. For many executives, earnings become a ritual. They write a script, create slides, and entertain questions. While ritualistic, this process provides activity rather than strategy. When earnings are treated as noise, they create volatility that exhausts and builds until the next quarter.

But it is not noise. Earnings are the operating system of the capital markets. Every other means of engagement – road shows, investor targeting, capital markets days, etc. – attach credibility to the engagement established by the earnings cycle. Analysts adopt or reject management's framework based on what is stated in earnings. Investors deploy capital with conviction or sell out in uncertainty based on how credulity is restored. Liquidity deepens or is lost based on how the system is designed.

Earnings are not limitations on the disclosure of results. They are the design architecture that disciplines management, teaches analysts, and contains investors. Companies that embrace them as operating systems have a tighter consensus, lower costs of capital, and maximize flexibility to raise capital and reinvest. Companies that disdain them have a permanent discount, no matter the fundamentals of their situation.

6.1. The Pre-Earnings Phase: Building the Design Architecture Before the Test

The most consequential work of an earnings cycle occurs before executives speak. Preparation determines whether a quarter reinforces credibility or breaks the cadence that sustains it.

Disclosure design is the leading edge of the architecture. Companies often try to cover too many metrics at once. Analysts are then forced to infer which variables actually matter, and volatility follows. The disciplined company starts with an audit to determine which operating variables explain most of the variance in cash generation over time, and it reports those variables consistently. For a retailer, that may be traffic, average basket size, and gross margin. For a software platform, it is often churn, net retention, and the unit economics that explain growth quality. Once the variables are defined, they should be disclosed with stable definitions and reconciled to GAAP so the market can trace operating reality into revenue, earnings, and cash flow. The objective is not more disclosure, it is more modelable disclosure.

Guidance calibration is equally essential. Overstretched guidance erodes trust faster than almost anything else. Markets pay for proof before promise. Guidance should therefore be calibrated to a plausible landscape, meaning the range of outcomes the market will consider given the company's historical forecasting error and the current environment. Repeated performance within a stated range builds credibility over time. Repeatedly stretching for an aspirational number, especially on margin, triggers lasting discounting because it changes how the market weights management's upside case.

Analyst education happens in the quiet period before the print. This is where advisors and investor relations teams align management on the few messages and variables that need to be reiterated, and where the reconciliation pathway is taught. Analysts need to learn not only what to model, but how to model it. When education is rushed or deferred, the market often defaults to crude proxies, and a consensus can form around the wrong drivers. Once that happens, it can take years of repeated proof to reset the model.

Competitor benchmarking also belongs in the pre-earnings phase. Investors will perform their own reality check through peer comparison, whether the company intends it or not. If a company's disclosure is weaker than peers' or lacks the same rigor as the star examples investors use as reference points, credibility can be impaired even when operational performance is strong in the moment. Management should anticipate how peers will disclose, underline where the company is leading, and be explicit about where differences in definitions or business models require a different set of metrics. Peer comparison is not cosmetic. It is part of how valuation multiples are set in practice.

All preparation for storytelling should be grounded in a targeting strategy. The weeks after an earnings event are the most consequential window for investor interest, which means the right owners must be identified in advance. If the story is reinvestment and long-term growth, the focus should be on growth-oriented funds with lower turnover that can underwrite a multi-quarter path. If the story is capital return and durability, income-oriented funds are the natural focus. Meeting new investors after an earnings event does not amplify a well-designed story. It often dilutes it by pulling management into explanations that should have been prepared before the test.

6.2. The Earnings Event: Credibility Test Under Relentless Public Discernment

The earnings call is not an accounting digest. It is a discipline test under relentless scrutiny. Executives must demonstrate the chosen variables, tie them to GAAP, and use consistent language to frame how the company is evolving. A growth company must show unit economics and the path to scale. A more mature company must demonstrate cash discipline, capital return, and the guardrails that protect durability. When management holds too tightly to the wrong frame, the result is narrative dissonance. A growth company speaks only in ambitions without showing the proof points that justify belief. A mature company borrows the language of growth while failing to show the cash discipline that earns a higher multiple. Sometimes these descriptions can apply to the same issuer at different moments, but the distinction is not cosmetic. It is the difference between a story that is underwriteable and one that is merely asserted.

Analyst questions influence outcomes almost as much as prepared remarks. Analysts who repeat the company's variables reinforce the architecture. Analysts who press for inconsistent or drifting disclosure undermine it. This is why pre-earnings education matters. Analysts are not neutral. They are the interpreters whose notes in the hours and days after the call establish consensus.

Tone matters as much as content. Overly promotional language creates narrative overhang, where aspiration is priced as risk rather than opportunity. Excessive caution can compress multiples by signaling uncertainty and drift. The middle ground is evidence-based ambition: proof first, promise second, sequenced over time.

6.3. The Post-Earnings Process: Reinforcement and Compounding

The call does not end the process. What happens in the weeks after earnings determines whether credibility compounds or decays.

Analyst adoption must be monitored closely. Advisors should review published notes to see whether analysts are repeating the intended drivers. When multiple notes converge on the same variables, the architecture is working. When notes cite competing variables, disclosure needs adjustment. This feedback loop is what reinforces architecture quarter after quarter.

Investor engagement begins post results. Roadshows, conferences, and one-on-one meetings should restate the same variables and show investors how those variables map to their mandates. When investors leave with the same language and the same model structure they heard on the call, the architecture compounds. When they hear new drivers or a shifting scorecard, trust fractures.

Performance and perception studies formalize the feedback process. Structured interviews with investors test whether disclosures are trusted, whether guidance is credible, and whether management is perceived as consistent. The findings should be pulled into the next earnings cycle. Without reinforcement, credibility dissipates between quarters.

Ownership assessment completes the loop. If the intended mandates are showing up in the shareholder base, turnover is falling, and holding periods are lengthening, the earnings system is creating stability. If the base shifts toward speculative holders and turnover increases, the system is failing, regardless of the quality of the prepared materials.

6.4. Case Studies in Earnings Architecture

Operating system principles are best demonstrated through live cases, where disclosure design either compounds credibility or imposes a cost. The cases below are based on publicly available disclosures and market behavior and are presented for illustrative purposes.

6.4.1. Apple: Evolving Its Narrative from Hardware to Ecosystem

For years, Apple disclosed iPhone unit sales and the market built models around product cycles with relatively consistent framing. When Apple later reduced emphasis on unit disclosures, analysts had to rely more heavily on revenue and mix, and the market's framing shifted toward questions of visibility and durability.

Over time, Apple reinforced an alternate disclosure architecture that emphasized revenue by category, services, and installed base-oriented indicators. The result was not a single metric replacement. It was a systematic shift toward ecosystem monetization and recurring behavior, disclosed with definitions that investors could revisit each quarter. The takeaway is that disclosure architecture can evolve, but it cannot simply remove a foundational variable without providing a modelable replacement. Abrupt changes create uncertainty. Sequenced change, paired with repeatable disclosure, can preserve credibility.

6.4.2. General Electric: The Transient Cost of Drift

GE illustrates how drift compounds when disclosure does not converge on a stable scorecard. In periods where divisional performance and guidance lacked clear, consistent framing, analyst estimates diverged, and valuation reflected a credibility discount.

In later periods, management narrowed the external scorecard, strengthened reconciliation to reported financials, and reset expectations in a more conservative posture consistent with rebuilding credibility. Over time, the market's models became more anchored, but the cost of prior drift did not reverse quickly. The broader lesson is that drift and overstatement are not cosmetic. They compound into structural discounting until repaired through disciplined, repeatable disclosure and delivery.

6.4.3. Netflix: Sequencing the Transition from Growth to Cash Flow

In Netflix's earlier growth phase, subscriber additions and churn were central drivers in models and valuation. As the business matured, those metrics alone became less explanatory for cash generation, and the market required a different set of variables to underwrite operating leverage and returns.

Management increasingly emphasized ARPU, engagement behavior, margin structure, and free cash flow trajectory, and repeated the revised framing across multiple quarters. Transition periods tend to produce volatility because the market is re learning the scorecard. The lesson is that disclosures must change with the stage, but the change must be sequenced. New variables must be defined, reconciled to GAAP, and reiterated until the market's model converges.

6.4.4. Uber: Complexity Without Taxonomy

At public market entry, Uber disclosed a wide range of metrics, including adjusted measures, and definitions evolved as the business model matured. When disclosure lacks hierarchy, analysts struggle to anchor valuation, and consensus can fragment. Volatility then reflects uncertainty as much as fundamentals.

Over time, the more effective approach is not maximal disclosure. It is taxonomy. A small set of primary variables, consistently defined and reconciled to GAAP, gives investors a model they can maintain across quarters. The takeaway is that complexity without hierarchy weakens the earnings system. Investors cannot model what they cannot reconcile.

6.4.5. Amazon: Profitless Growth to a Focus on Returns

For years, investors debated Amazon's willingness to convert scale into durable profitability. The disclosures showed revenue expansion, but the market's debate centered on whether operating leverage and returns would become visible and measurable.

Over time, Amazon provided clearer segmentation and profitability framing, including greater visibility into AWS economics and operating income dynamics by business line. As investors gained a more modelable framework for returns alongside reinvestment, the debate shifted from whether margins would exist to how they would scale. The lesson is that segmentation and return orientation can change the market's underwriting posture when the disclosures make profitability legible rather than hypothetical.

6.4.6. JPMorgan: Stability as Premium

JPMorgan illustrates earnings as a stable operating system. Guidance and framing tend to concentrate on a small set of variables that investors can track through cycles, including core profitability drivers and capital strength. The call structure is consistent, definitions are stable, and performance is repeatedly anchored to the same scorecard.

Post-call engagement reinforces the same framing for long-horizon owners who prize predictability. Over time, that consistency can support a valuation premium because the market is paying for reduced uncertainty. For mature companies, the objective is not to generate excitement. It is to produce confidence through repeatable proof.

6.5. Earnings as Governance

Earnings are not quarterly noise. They are governance mechanisms for credibility. They supervise management by tying ambition to evidence. They inform analysts by exposing them to reconciled variables, as they need to know why. They form investor conviction by evidencing or precluding the narrative through the delivery of the results.

The ones that win are the ones that design this system with purpose. They make disclosures that identify true products, calibrate guidance within established credibility curves, educate analysts with a plausible alternative, and align with deluded parallels. They treat the call as a discipline performance displaying tone and content. They extend credibility after the call by targeting reputational studies and ownership studies. They repeat preposterously until credibility is cultivated.

Earnings are the operating system of capital markets. They are what create whether an investor believes, whether analysts center on the share price, reduce volatility, and stop. Ultimately, valuation is not just what a company earns. It's how the company teaches the market to believe what they earn.

Chapter 7.
Perception and Sentiment Audits

Perception studies and sentiment audits are not reflections of management's message. They are diagnostic tools that reveal what the market has actually internalized. They test whether analyst models align with intended drivers. They show whether investors accept guidance and whether governance is seen as a source of risk or reinforcement. They uncover whether peers have claimed narrative territory that the company believed it controlled.

Most importantly, they translate qualitative interpretation into actionable outcomes for valuation, liquidity, and cost of capital. When conducted rigorously, they become the control system for the operating cadence set in earnings. When conducted superficially as surveys or quick pulses, they create noise and false confidence.

Perception is not opinion. In capital markets, it is the set of structured beliefs embedded in models, investment committees, and risk budgets. Sentiment is not mood. It is the direction and intensity of probability weights investors assign to future outcomes. Good audits address both and translate the findings into changes in disclosure, targeting, and sequencing. Bad audits mistake politeness for conviction, report what respondents think management wants to hear, and fail to assess the underlying beliefs that move price.

7.1. The role of diagnostic work in the operating system

Earnings define cadence. Perception audits determine if that cadence is teaching the market what the company intends. Without diagnostics, management assumes that disclosure needs equal adoption. In reality, adoption occurs when analysts redo their models using your selected variables, when the coverage language starts to demonstrate your selected architecture, and when investors who have aligned mandates underwrite that selected architecture with capital. Diagnostics are in between intent and adoption. They observe the observers. They uncover the gaps. They demand that management teams grapple with how the market actually reasons from a business standpoint.

This diagnostic could be employed at three instances. Before a major shift in disclosure or strategy, diagnostics check if the market is ready to start teaching new drivers. During a period of uncertainty, diagnostics can identify whether the source of volatility is misunderstanding or repricing risk. After a cycle of grading disclosures, diagnostics will demonstrate whether credibility is compounding and where to go next. In all instances, a diagnostic is not a report folder. It's a decision-making document that informs the next quarter's architecture.

7.2. Developing a valid audience perception study

A valid study starts with the audience. The purpose is not to talk to everyone. It is to speak to those agents who enable the marginal price. The target must seek out analysts who discuss models that form the consensus, long-only institutions, and fundamental hedge funds that provide long-term holdings, and marginal buyers who move prices in distress. Look to include investors who are eager to flesh out contradictory evidence. Also, a passive fund will be included if governance or index inclusion is pertinent to the risk. A study that features too many generalists or conference buddies will document chatter and not price discovery. This instrument is a semi-structured interview guide to elicit modeling behavior, trust formation, and peer framing. The questions explore which operating variables respondents actually model, how they reconcile those variables to GAAP, what noise they identify, what risk they feel management took too lightly, which peers are invoked for the valuation set, and what would need to be disclosed for an increase or decrease in position size. Respondents describe their last model change and walk through the corresponding line items. They rank the credibility of the guidance ranges, not in a five-point form, but in basis points of risk premium taken on or taken off the last two quarters. They describe management's tone for the last three calls and whether that tone raised or lowered expectations for this period.

Fieldwork quality control is important. Interviews need to be blinded to management where appropriate, time-bound (to avoid fatigue), and conducted by professionals who understand buy-side and sell-side incentives. Responses are recorded, transcribed, and coded independently by two analysts to mitigate the effects of interpretive bias. Disconfirming evidence is privileged. If nine respondents use management's language, and three credible respondents reject it for the same reason, the diagnostic must privilege that dissent, not average it away.

Analysis translates raw language to architecture. Coding does not count adjectives. It maps mental models. Coding is used to determine what scale variables sit in their models, and if they match those pointed to by the Company. If respondents indicate governance concerns, the coding indicates whether that is board independence, incentive design, related-party exposure, or none of that. If respondents reference peers, the coding indicates the peer set they are implying and the vectors of comparison. The result is a codified view of how the market is thinking. It is not a collage of quotes. It is a codified model of models.

The evidence is a decision document, not a slide deck. It isolates relevance in the Company's architecture, where adopted and rejected, and why. It states which variables stay in the next cycle's supporting evidence, which disclosures are more GAAP aligned, which segments of guidance are recast to the credibility curve, and which investors must be prioritized because their beliefs are already aligned with the Company's story. A sequence is prescribed to introduce new variables, so proof comes before promise. It identifies the sentences in coverage notes that need to be changed and which comparative tables must move to another set of peers.

7.3. Around building a sentiment audit that captures market signals

Perception work is qualitative and deep. Sentiment work is integrative and continuous. An accurate sentiment audit weaves together four channels. The first is analyst commentary and distribution. With each earnings cycle, the audit observes if coverage notes reflect the variables management chooses, the accuracy of estimates converges around those variables, and price targets reference the new peer set or the old peer set. The second is ownership structure and turnover. The audit observes what mandates are adding or trimming, what hold periods are like per mandates, and whether the marginal buyer in volatility respects the story. The third is market microstructure. Bid-ask spreads, order book depth, and event day slippage are all monitored because these are where credibility meets liquidity. The fourth is peer-relative changes. If peers who offer certain metrics are rewarded and the company is not offering those metrics, the audit reveals a competitive disclosure gap.

A sentiment audit does not produce a dashboard. It establishes a rhythm of Bayesian updating. Every quarter, the company reconfirms its beliefs on what the market has learned and not learned. If analysts repeatedly ask about a metric for which management considers secondary, management must either defend why the metric is secondary with reconciliation and evidence or accept that the market will discount it until management expresses a better metric. If long-only holders reduce after a credible beat, the audit examines whether mandates were misinterpreted. If the bid-ask spreads widen around calls, the audit investigates whether the ranges were too wide to de-risk the event.

7.4. Embedding diagnostics into the earnings rhythm

Diagnostics are only valuable if they change behavior. The most common failure is to read an audit, nod in agreement, and then run the next quarter exactly the same. Embedding means treating it as part of the earnings preparation checklist. Before guidance is agreed, the leadership team reviews which disclosures were adopted, which were dropped, and which raised the most credibility concerns. Guidance ranges are then modified to reflect the credibility curve signaled by the market, not the internal aspirations of the operating team. The document is sequenced so that adopted items appear up front and tie more directly to GAAP, while risks investors already recognize are clearly addressed. Q&A rehearsal includes audit-type questions, not just friendly ones. The post-earnings roadshow is re-planned so that the first meetings are with mandates that the audit shows to be most aligned and effective.

The same embedding applies after the call. Research notes are read not for tone, but for the architecture of their arguments. If two influential analysts continue to frame the business through yesterday's story, management immediately re-engages them with a focused teach-in and addresses the missing barrier. If coverage appropriately repositions the peer table to the company's advantage, management reinforces that shift with comparative disclosures in the next quarter. If a subset of holders expresses skepticism about guidance, management narrows the range in the following quarter and demonstrates discipline in staying within it.

Embedding means treating diagnostic signals as operational priorities, not as commentary.

7.4.1. Case study: Apple and the disciplined rebuild of belief

Context: For years, Apple supported market underwriting with a stable set of operating and financial anchors. Analysts built forecasting frameworks around product cycles, margin dynamics, and repeatable guidance framing, and coverage language converged around a familiar hardware model.

Disclosure gap: When Apple later reduced emphasis on unit disclosures, the market lost a legacy variable that had served as a central scaffold for modeling. In the absence of a fully taught replacement scorecard, analysts leaned more heavily on narrative proxies, and the framing drifted toward cyclical hardware interpretations, even as fundamentals continued to be debated through revenue and margin.

Diagnostic sequence: A disciplined approach requires designing the replacement architecture before removing the legacy variable, then introducing the new variables in sequence and reinforcing them through repetition. Over time, Apple increasingly emphasized an alternate scorecard centered on services revenue, installed base-oriented indicators, and ecosystem monetization, supported by stable definitions and reconciliation to GAAP categories that investors could model.

Outcome: The market's language gradually shifted from unit-centric models toward an ecosystem framing once the replacement variables became repeatable and modelable. The takeaway is strict. Disclosure architectures can evolve, but removal without a modelable replacement creates a credibility break. Sequenced substitution, paired with repeated disclosure, is how credibility is preserved.

7.4.2. Case Study: General Electric and the long remediation of drift

Context: Over extended periods, GE's external framing was complicated by shifting definitions, expansive segment narratives, and guidance that did not consistently converge into a stable market scorecard. Analyst models diverged, and investor interpretation reflected uncertainty about which variables were primary.

Disclosure gap: When disclosure does not settle on a small, repeatable set of drivers, consensus fragments. The observable symptoms are widening estimate dispersion, recurring debate over the scorecard, and event-day volatility that reflects credibility risk as much as operating performance.

Diagnostic sequence: Remediation begins when leadership narrows the external scorecard, resets expectations within a credible curve, and strengthens reconciliation to reported financials. Diagnostics act as a metronome by testing whether the new variables are not only heard but adopted, which can be observed through convergence in language, reduced dispersion, and increased participation from longer-horizon mandates willing to underwrite multi-quarter repair.

Outcome: Credibility penalties do not reverse quickly. Each quarter of delivery within the credible curve pays down the penalty incrementally. The issuer that measures adoption and adjusts cadence and disclosure design remediates faster than the issuer that assumes the market will relearn on its own.

Case study: Netflix and the shift from subscribers to cash

Context: In Netflix's growth phase, subscriber additions and churn served as the dominant underwriting variables. As maturity approached, subscriber metrics became less explanatory for cash generation and operating leverage, and the market required a revised scorecard.

Disclosure gap: Transition periods create model conflict. Parts of the Street remain anchored to legacy growth variables while others attempt to incorporate new drivers such as ARPU, engagement, and margin structure. Without disciplined sequencing, the market oscillates between frameworks, and volatility becomes a function of contested interpretation rather than new information.

Diagnostic sequence: A disciplined sequence introduces the revised variables, defines them tightly, reconciles them to GAAP outcomes, and repeats them over multiple quarters until the market's language converges. Management must also reinforce the time horizon, aligning engagement toward owners who can underwrite a cash generation transition rather than only near-term subscriber optics.

Outcome: The market learns new architectures through repetition. The lesson is that disclosures must evolve with the stage, but the evolution must be sequenced. New variables must become modelable and repeatable, or the market will stay split and keep pricing uncertainty.

7.4.3. Case study: Uber and the charm of complexity without hierarchy

Context: Uber entered public markets with a complex set of operating metrics, including adjusted measures, and definitions evolved as the business model matured. Analysts approached the name with different hierarchies for what mattered most.

Disclosure gap: Complexity without taxonomy fragments models. Some analysts center on bookings, others on revenue constructs, others on contribution margin or adjusted profitability. When the hierarchy is unclear and reconciliation is weak, consensus diverges, and event volatility rises because the market cannot anchor valuation to a common model.

Diagnostic sequence: The diagnostic is to identify the point of confusion and then restore hierarchy. A small set of primary drivers, consistently defined and reconciled to GAAP, must be elevated above secondary indicators. Repetition matters more than breadth. The aim is to make the model maintainable across quarters.

Outcome: Stability improves when investors can converge on a shared scorecard. The inference is simple. When the market does not know which variables matter most, it prices the company with a volatility premium. Diagnostics have value only if they lead to simplification, reconciliation, and repeated disclosure.

7.4.4. Case in point: Tesla during the Model 3 ramp

Context: During the Model 3 ramp, Tesla was underwritten through two competing architectures. One emphasized scale, learning curves, and margin trajectory. The other emphasized liquidity, execution risk, and near-term financing constraints. The marginal buyer shifted as each framework gained or lost narrative dominance.

Disclosure gap: When two architectures coexist, the stock becomes a referendum on which framework investors choose to believe. Without repeatable evidence that allows one model to dominate, pricing behavior becomes episodic, and volatility reflects shifting ownership rather than a stable underwriting base.

Diagnostic sequence: The diagnostic sequence is to protect the primary architecture with repeatable proof points and to align engagement toward mandates willing to underwrite that path. As output and margin trajectory become more legible through consistent reporting and delivery cadence, longer-horizon owners can backstop the dominant framework through noise, and coverage language can begin to converge around the same variables.

Outcome: Stability emerges when one architecture wins and becomes the market's routine model. The lesson is not that every mandate must be won. The issuer that tries to speak to all mandates dilutes its own scorecard. The issuer that makes a prioritized architecture modelable and repeatedly proven earns greater credibility and, with it, greater stability.

7.4.5. Case study: A sovereign issuer and the disciplined use of sentiment

Context: Sovereigns face the same credibility mechanics, expressed through spreads and buyer composition. Ahead of a new bond program, such as an ESG-linked issuance, the sovereign must anticipate whether investors will trust the framework enough to price it.

Disclosure gap: ESG-designated capital requires verifiability. Investors need confidence that the use of proceeds will be traceable, the reporting cadence will meet institutional standards, and verification will be viewed as independent and resilient to political cycles. Without those elements, the market embeds a credibility premium and demand narrows.

Diagnostic sequence: Diagnostics combine structured market feedback with observable spread behavior relative to comparable issuers. The sovereign must test trust thresholds in advance, then design a framework that meets them through governance, reporting cadence, and verification standards. The framework must be repeatable, not episodic, and it must allow investors to return to it over time.

Outcome: When the framework is credible, and reporting is consistent, the buyer set can broaden and pricing can improve. When doubts persist, spreads reflect a credibility discount. The lesson generalizes to corporations. Credibility in a new disclosure category is established by pre-testing the market's trust threshold and meeting it with design, evidence, and cadence.

7.5. Creating Diagnostics for Diagnosis

The audit only matters if it changes the next steps. The work with the leadership team is straightforward. Did the last perception study make disclosure simpler or more obvious? Did it change the guidance range? Did it alter the order of the script so that evidence came before aspiration? Did it shape the first ten conversations after earnings? Did it affect the peer group table on slide three? Did it prevent an avoidable surprise by forcing the team to address a risk the market had already priced in, but the script ignored?

The most sophisticated teams add one more layer. They treat the audit as a running series, not a single episode. They document the market's beliefs about the business quarter by quarter. They track how quickly those beliefs shift in response to evidence. They identify which investors are belief leaders and which are belief followers. They prioritize scarce leadership attention accordingly. They view perception not as an opinion poll, but as a map of price formation.

7.6. Diagnosis as a Discipline

Perception and sentiment audits close the circle on what a company discloses and what the market believes. They do not flatter. They reveal the gap between disclosure and adoption, intention and interpretation, narrative and model. They cemented in the operational cadence of earnings elimination asymmetry, decreased dispersion, and directed capital to the hands most likely to stabilize valuation. If ignored or done superficially, they allow blind spots to become discounts.

A company cannot govern the market. A company can govern how it educates the market to think. Diagnosis is a tool to determine if the lesson has been learned. The work is repetitive, it is technical, and sometimes painful. It is also the work that will differentiate companies that compound their credibility from those that rely on chance with valuation.

Chapter 8. Connecting Narrative to Cost of Capital

Cost of capital is the value assigned to faith. It is reflected in equity risk premia, credit spreads, and liquidity premia, and from there it drives everything from strategies to market share. Companies with the same fundamentals can face vastly different costs of capital. The difference is that one has trained the market to ingest, trust, and underwrite its cash flow, while the other has not. Narrative explains the separation. It is not marketing, but the infrastructure that converts evidence into lower perceived risk.

Investors do not trade adjectives. They trade variance. If a company can show that the variables driving free cash flow to owners are persistent, observable, and within management's control, while distinguishing them from variables that are random or stochastic, the margin of safety demanded by investors declines. Multiples expand, yield, and the company gains new strategic latitude as free cash flow contributes more directly to value. In contrast, if a company is ambiguous, redefines variables, or offers speculation without evidence, investors will increase the premia they demand. The fundamentals may be the same, but valuation falls, reinvestment is rationed, and capital becomes more expensive.

This chapter makes that translation explicit. It shows how narrative maps directly onto components of the equity risk premium, how governance narrative influences credit spreads, how disclosure structure shapes estimate dispersion and beta, and how targeting determines the marginal buyer when liquidity is thin. It then applies the methodology to real cases where the cost of capital was reduced through a disciplined narrative or raised through a narrative overhang.

8.1. How narrative reduces the price of risk

The equity risk premium compensates for uncertainty in future cash flows. The equity risk premium is not a single number. The equity risk premium is a sum of beliefs about drivers' volatility, model error, agency and governance risk, and crisis behavior. Narrative contributes to each. Generally, when a firm presents a stable collection of operations variables and reconciles with GAAP consistently without drift, investors can conclude low model error and low agency reporting. When guidance is calibrated within a known credibility curve and then provided, investors will reduce the probability weight they assign to tail results. When governance narrative requires specifics about capital discipline, incentives, and board independence, investors will reduce the expected agency cost. In each case, narrative lowers those premiums without convincing, but by offering some evidence that better informs and reduces uncertainty.

Credit spreads are also the same story on the downside. Lenders do not model upside. Lenders model resilience. Lenders ask themselves about covenants, cash coverage through cycles, and management behavior to avoid subordinating them unexpectedly. Governance narrative in concert with policy and history lowers those perceived risks. This is also why the same issuer is able to issue at more competitive rates after years of stable reporting and conservative delivery, even if top-line growth has not changed.

Market microstructure displays the same behavior in real time. When an issuer's disclosure causes analysts to land on the same variable, the distribution of estimates becomes narrower, event day trading volume contracts, and order book increases. Reduced slippage and narrower spreads are not marketing. They are the trail left by a lower perceived risk in the market.

8.2. A way to convert a story into a spread

Good discipline among advisors starts with variance decomposition. The objective is to quantify which operational variables truly drive fluctuations in free cash flow. If the business is a payment network, the proper drivers may be corridor volume growth, stability of take rate by product, and operating leverage from variable platform costs. If the business is a renewable developer, the appropriate claimed drivers are contracted cash flows, counterparty quality, tenor, and execution risk by stage. The decomposition is practical, over a range of quarters and cycles, not the long list of metrics companies usually bring to every call.

Once the drivers are recognized, the narrative is formed around their evidence of control. Each narrative claim is correlated to a disclosure that is readily auditable. For example, a claim about pricing power links with disclosure on elasticities, churn, and cohort behavior linked to revenue. A claim about defensibility links to disclosures on renewal rates, switching costs, and contracts linked to cash flow. A claim about discipline links to disclosures on hurdle rates and actual capital allocation decisions linked to returns.

Governance follows the same logic. Investors need to see how incentives meet long-run value add and how capital may be returned or retained. The narrative links to the policy, the disclosure demonstrates that policy is followed, and with each delivery, credibility builds through multiple cycles. Capital cost implications are scarcely speculative. As drivers' uncertainty diminishes, the premium for holding cash flows diminishes.

Adoption is measurable. Perception interviews test whether analysts have rebuilt their models around the selected variables and whether investors describe risk using the company's intended language. Sentiment audits track dispersion, event volatility, peer relative performance, and spread behavior. When adoption is absent, do not escalate the promise. Reinforce reconciliation, recalibrate guidance to a credible curve, and repeat until the market signals learning through observable behavior.

8.2.1. Case example: Amazon and sustained skepticism

For much of its public life, Amazon was framed by skeptics as profitless growth. The outline was simple. Revenue scaled, while reported profitability was restrained by reinvestment. The market debate centered on whether durable margins would materialize or whether they would appear only at the expense of growth. That belief functioned as a credibility discount and raised the implied equity risk premium embedded in valuation.

Reframing progressed as the company emphasized variables tied to cash creation and provided greater segmentation. Investors were increasingly able to separate the economics of retail reinvestment from profitability in higher margin categories such as AWS, and to underwrite operating leverage as a function of business mix and maturity rather than as an article of faith. Over multiple quarters, the critical work was consistent. The disclosures were repeatedly tied back to GAAP categories, and the narrative leaned on reconciliation rather than marketing.

As segmentation and repeatable variables took hold, coverage language shifted. Research increasingly treated AWS as an engine with its own margin trajectory, and models reflected a portfolio view of heterogeneous businesses rather than a single opaque block. Longer-horizon investors could then underwrite those returns, and growth could coexist because the path to returns had become auditable, not merely asserted. The general lesson is that when the company itself is a portfolio, capital pricing tends to reflect the least understood component unless disclosure makes the true drivers legible and keeps them stable enough to be modeled without drift.

8.2.2. Case study: WeWork and pricing under narrative overhang

WeWork attempted to fund growth with a narrative that could not be modeled into cash flow with sufficient discipline. In private markets, enthusiasm from a concentrated group of buyers can sustain premium pricing for longer than fundamentals would justify. In public markets, feedback is less forgiving. When the operating model cannot be connected to unit economics and cash generation in a way that survives scrutiny, the gap between aspiration and evidence is priced as risk. When governance questions are central, required returns rise further because uncertainty is no longer only operational.

Public filing did not resolve the core questions. It elevated concerns about losses, governance structure, and the plausibility of a credible path to sustainable economics. Without a stable set of underwriteable variables, analysts could not construct a valuation framework that institutional investors could defend in committee. Capital, when available, demanded terms that would have challenged the economics of the model.

The salvage lesson is not moral; it is mechanical. Overhang is reduced by narrowing claims to what can be proven. Substantiate unit economics in a representative subset, lock in more durable customer economics, repair governance credibility, and then broaden the claim only after the proof points have been repeated. Absent that sequence, the market will price the uncertainty so aggressively that scalable financing becomes impractical.

8.2.3. Case study: Mexico sovereign ESG bond and the integrity of frameworks

Sovereigns are priced across many dimensions, but weakness in the framework around labeled proceeds can create a credibility premium that shows up in pricing. When Mexico introduced a sovereign labeled framework in 2019, the macro fundamentals did not change overnight. What changed was the disclosure architecture around the use of proceeds and reporting. The sovereign published a sustainable finance framework that identified eligible projects, governance for selection, reporting cadence, and external review. That structure reduced mandate risk for investors sensitive to greenwashing concerns because it made verification and ongoing monitoring more feasible.

Demand for labeled issuances is ultimately a function of trust, not marketing. When a framework is auditable and reporting is repeatable, incremental pools of capital can participate with greater confidence, and pricing can reflect reduced uncertainty and broader demand. The corporate analogy is direct. New categories of disclosure or financing do not earn premiums on goodwill. Markets reward frameworks that are verifiable and replicable. Without that ecosystem, skeptical mandates apply a credibility discount.

8.2.4. Case study: Exxon Mobil and the governance risk premium

For years, portions of the market viewed Exxon Mobil's approach to climate governance and capital allocation oversight as slow to evolve. Even investors who respected operating performance often embedded a governance-related risk premium, reflecting beliefs about board oversight, incentive design, and the company's willingness to adapt capital allocation to long-run risk.

Changes to governance signaling, including board composition shifts and subsequent adjustments in disclosure and capital allocation framing, did not simplify the underlying operational complexity. They did, however, alter risk beliefs for investors who treat governance as an underwriting variable. In that sense, credibility moved not on speeches, but on governance mechanisms that modified perceived agency risk and changed the probability distribution investors assign to capital allocation outcomes.

The takeaway is that governance is not an ethics discussion in capital markets. It is a pricing variable. When boards and incentives reduce perceived agency risk, both equity and credit investors tend to reduce the premiums they require, particularly during periods when governance is under active scrutiny.

8.2.5. Case study: JPMorgan and the structure of a stability premium

Some issuers earn a premium because stability itself is the product. JPMorgan illustrates this dynamic. Over time, guidance has tended to be calibrated conservatively, disclosure has been consistent, and management has delivered within framed ranges often enough that investors treat guidance as probabilistic rather than aspirational. In stress periods, the narrative is repeatedly reality checked through a focus on resilience, capital strength, and risk controls rather than on promotional growth claims.

The benefits show up in the mandate fit. Long-horizon owners who prize stability are more willing to hold through volatility, and credit markets often reflect lower uncertainty when risk controls and disclosure are viewed as credible and timely. The bank’s cost of capital is not anchored only to growth. It is supported by the investor's belief that downside risk is monitored and that disclosure will arrive early enough to be actionable.

The playbook is straightforward. Set ranges that can be defended, disclose the variables that govern capital adequacy and returns, correct without drift, and respond to shocks in a grounded way that reinforces the scorecard. Over time, the market will price the difference.

8.3. From a narrative design to a metrics premium

The operational playbook is linear in function; first, define the few variables that actually impact free cash flow, and then quantify the variance over the cycles. The second design disclosure is for outsiders to map those variables in a transparent way that leads back to GAAP results. That's the third one, calibrated guidance within the credibility curve that can really happen. Fourth, governance narratives should be reflected in policies, incentives, and board composition, and should be supported by concrete actions—even at the expense of higher costs. Fifth, investors should ensure their objectives are closely aligned with those of the company so that even during market fluctuations, marginal buyers can remain engaged. Sixth, leveraging adoption with disciplined diagnostics creates adjustments without the drama. The cost of capital will follow once the market can reduce the uncertainty it requires to price it.

This is nothing soft. It puts management teams in a position of facing what they can control and what they can't, willingly relinquish rhetorical space for trust, and speak explicitly about the truth that credibility is earned or lost in the first quarter of a day. It's more than just a higher multiple reward; it is the opportunity to spend capital well, outlive competition, and compound return.

8.4. Changing beliefs into basis points

The cost of capital is a reflection of credibility. The narratives change that realization for the better by rationalizing certainty to the future cash drivers and expected management behavior. Those who do so with discipline change their beliefs into basis points. They get capital at rates and terms their competition cannot, they invest over or around cycles, and they come out of a crisis stronger than they went in. Crooked narratives have a penalty on capital that further supports unwelcome scrutiny every time they look for capital.

The ultimate credibility test is: if you were to stop disclosing measures today, would the street credibly model your business? If yes, you have blended your story and cost of capital. Then blended is the value work.

Chapter 9.
Execution Cases

9.1. Recovery: reinstating credibility following a crisis

9.1.1. What markets price in a crisis

Crises reprice/assess the cost of money faster than they impair operations. Equity investors widen the discount rate when they are uncertain; they can forecast with confidence. Debt investors widen spreads when the path to repayment appears uncertain or governance appears weak. In equity, you can see these three ways. First, realized and implied volatility spikes and beta rises, which increase your cost of equity even if long-term growth is unchanged. Second, analyst dispersion increases, suggesting the street is guessing rather than modeling. Third, liquidity quality declines with increased price impact for the same notional traded and a noticeable decline in closing auction depth. In credit, you see a similar pattern. CDS widens before ratings changes. New issue concessions increase. Covenants tighten, and maturities shorten.

The point is straightforward. In a crisis, investors are not punishing revenue. They are punishing uncertainty. If you credibly mitigate uncertainty, the market will decrease the premium (or required return) it charges you, well before all operational metrics are back to normal.

9.1.2. The advisory approach that facilitates recovery

There is a sequence that reliably restores credibility. It is not theater; it is a technical reconstruction of how, and from where, the market is modeling the company.

Stabilize the information flow. Within the first seventy-two hours, determine what the company must file, what it must correct, and what it must not speculate upon publicly. Set a single cadence for updates, name accountable owners, and eliminate unscripted commentary that compounds risk and becomes part of the discovery record. If legal or regulatory constraints restrict what may be stated, clarify the constraint and keep the cadence nevertheless. Markets can tolerate less information when cadence and accountability exist.

Diagnose variance. Assemble five to twelve quarters of clean operating and financial data at the most granular detail possible. Reverse any definition drift. Run a hierarchy of simple tests rather than an academic experiment. Start with additive bridge logic that shows contributions to variance in free cash flow. Check whether the correlations are stable over time. Use sparse regression only to identify the minimal set of drivers, not to fit the past. If the algorithm identifies seven variables, you have not diagnosed the business; you have overfit. Stop when two to four drivers account for nearly all movement in free cash flow, and you can articulate those drivers in plain English to a portfolio manager in ten minutes or less.

Build a disclosure architecture from those drivers. Every credible recovery performs the same three moves. It precisely defines each metric in the 10 Q, or equivalent primary disclosure, and locks the definitions for the next eight quarters. It reconciles operating drivers to GAAP revenue, operating income, cash conversion, and leverage, so analysts can carry numbers through models without inventing bridges. It provides proof over time through a milestone ladder that integrates leading indicators and hard outcomes. The leading indicators show a trend. The hard outcomes confirm the trend in cash.

Calibrate guidance within the credibility curve. The market assigns a believable range to each management team based on its track record. Guide within that range and achieve it consistently, and the range widens while the credibility premium drops. Guide out of range and miss, and the range shrinks while the premium rises. Decide what variables to guide, what to answer qualitatively, and what to let models infer. Address the one factor that side risk committees lose sleep over and deliberately reduce it. That could be liquidity headroom, covenant headroom, or a capacity bottleneck.

Educate the Street on how to model you. Do not drown analysts in minor caveats. Provide a concise model logic that works with your disclosures and can be carried into a spreadsheet without interpretive gymnastics. Stress it in the deck, the script, the Q and A, and every post-call follow-up. Reinforce it in small groups with lead analysts and sector generalists, because consensus language is built in these rooms before it is formalized.

Reconstruct the register. Track who sold into the drawdown, who bought the first rebound, and who is holding for duration. Segment by mandate, turnover, position concentration, and recovery history in your sector. Reset the roadshow and conference mix toward long-only holders who can endure multi-quarter repair. Lead with the CFO and the operating executive responsible for the deciding metric, and replace momentum dialogue with driver dialogue. If a holder is insistent on a catalyst you will not meet, let it go. Stability is a function of aligned mandates, not more meetings.

Operate the feedback loop as a process. Each quarter, gather four signals and put them on one page for leadership and the board. The first is analyst dispersion, including the tails. The second is the language and structure of lead models, showing whether the drivers you are teaching are becoming consensus drivers. The third is ownership quality reflected in turnover, concentration, and mandate fit. The fourth is the credit spread curve relative to the equity multiple, showing whether governance credibility is being priced consistently across the capital structure. Decide what will change in the next quarter's disclosures before presentation polish expands the deck.

This sequence is not cosmetic. It is what allows an investor to take duration risk on you again. As the process reduces uncertainty, valuation can begin to recalibrate before operations fully recover.

9.1.2.1. Case 1. Chipotle: retail reconsideration via simplicity

Chipotle's 2015 crisis produced a rapid breakdown in trust. Traffic and same-store sales declined, public scrutiny intensified, and investors were forced to underwrite an outcome with limited visibility. The buy side is split into two broad postures. One assumed lasting brand impairment and embedded lower terminal economics. The other assumed a multi-year repair and modeled a recovery in traffic and margins. The result was not a neat midpoint. It was a widening dispersion, which functions as a credibility premium within the equity risk premium.

The work that mattered began with removing noise. Dozens of metrics were discussed across the ecosystem, but only a small subset was explanatory for cash generation. A disciplined variance review pointed to three drivers that carried most of the signal. Same store sales. Average check. Restaurant-level margin, which captured execution, cost, and operational control. In a recovery, the market does not reward a long scorecard. It rewards a scorecard that explains cash.

Disclosure then centered on those drivers. The variables were presented with stable definitions in public materials and referenced consistently across the earnings script and Q&A. Each driver was tied to GAAP outcomes through clean bridges so analysts could carry them through models without inventing assumptions or changing definitions to make forecasts work. The commitment was not simply to disclose. It was to disclose the same way, repeatedly, even when cosmetic changes could have created short-term perception benefits.

Guidance and proof points were sequenced around what could be shown, not what could be promised. Rather than offering a precise recovery timetable, management emphasized the next verifiable data points and calibrated forward expectations to an operational plan the market could observe. Leading indicators preceded hard outcomes, and the cadence created a learning loop. Over time, analyst questions shifted from whether recovery was possible to how quickly the variables were improving, and whether margin progression was durable as promotional activity normalized.

Targeting also mattered. Engagement weighted toward owners with experience underwriting branded consumer recoveries and a willingness to carry a multi-quarter pathway through volatility. Investors who required a near-term catalyst rotated out. Investors aligned with the driver framework became more central to the base. The goal was not consensus optimism. There was a consensus on the model.

Valuation began to respond as dispersion narrowed and the market converged on the same compact scorecard. The lesson is not that three drivers are a magic number. The lesson is that simplicity, reconciliation, and cadence reduce uncertainty premia in retail recoveries.

9.1.2.2. Case 2. Unilever: governance recovery through accountable structure

Unilever's 2018 headquarters proposal created a governance credibility issue, particularly among certain UK-focused holders who interpreted the move as raising questions about shareholder protections and accountability. The proposal was withdrawn, but governance damage rarely clears in a single act. Unlike a product failure, a governance episode is a capital markets event. Investors are underwriting future decision rights, board discipline, and how capital will be deployed under stress.

Governance recovery follows a different subject matter, but a similar structure. The skeptical holder is usually asking two practical questions. What commitments will constrain decision-making going forward, and who is accountable for enforcing them? How will those commitments translate into capital allocation and returns?

The disclosure response is to formalize oversight and make it repeatable. That can mean codifying the hierarchy of cash uses, clarifying the board's role in capital allocation guardrails, and committing to a reporting cadence that allows investors to test whether the policy is being followed. The engagement response is to put accountable governance figures in the room, not only executives delivering performance. When chair leadership and independent oversight are demonstrably engaged, the "who enforces" question becomes more answerable than it is through press language alone.

Over time, coverage language can shift away from structural uncertainty and back toward operating performance and capital returns if the accountability architecture is stable and observable. The key takeaway is that governance repair is not achieved through more expressive reassurances. It is achieved by changing the accountability mechanism around the levers of the market prices, and then reporting against that mechanism with discipline.

9.1.2.3. Case 3. BP post Macondo: energy recovery via balance sheet, safety, and legal architecture

The Deepwater Horizon event in 2010 created a compound crisis for BP: environmental damage, cash flow pressure, legal overhang, and a credibility challenge tied to operational risk. Both equity and credit were forced to price uncertainty, and traditional investor relations messaging alone was insufficient because the market was underwriting tail risk across multiple dimensions.

Recovery required parallel frameworks that addressed distinct premia. The balance sheet pillar had to be legible. Asset sale targets, leverage objectives, and dividend policy needed to be framed against conservative assumptions and reported consistently. The legal pillar had to be structural rather than rhetorical. Dedicated mechanisms for claims and liability management were required to reduce uncertainty about the magnitude, timing, and containment of obligations. The operational pillar needed to be anchored in safety governance. Investors needed evidence that safety oversight had authority that was independent enough to be credible, and that reporting cadence distinguished safety performance from production performance so incentives could be interpreted as durable.

Disclosure around these pillars needed to follow the recovery sequence. Definitions had to be concrete and stable. Reconciliations had to be transparent. Milestones had to be stated as ladders the market could follow, rather than as adjectives about intent. Engagement with long-only energy holders and crossover credit investors had to be anchored on those ladders rather than on optimism.

In complex legal overhangs, credit markets often respond earlier than equity because liability containment and balance sheet visibility can be priced before the full operational narrative is rehabilitated. Over time, as uncertainty is reduced rung by rung, both the breadth of assumptions embedded in equity and the risk premia embedded in credit can narrow. The lesson is that in multi-faceted crises, recovery requires parallel architectures. A balance sheet ladder does not eliminate legal uncertainty. A legal framework does not eliminate operational risk. Each premium must be reduced with its own disclosure and governance mechanism, repeated until the market has fewer reasons to price surprise.

Cross-Industry Adjustments that Matter

Retail and restaurants tend to hinge on traffic, check, and unit-level margins. Recovery architecture works best when it commits to those levers explicitly and resists the temptation to add a rotating metric of the month.

Tech issuers are often punished less for an isolated event and more for weak unit economics visibility. The drivers that matter typically include retention, cohort monetization, and customer acquisition efficiency, disclosed in a way that can be reconciled to financial statements so the story is modelable rather than rhetorical.

Industrials often recover on backlog quality and cash conversion. Order intake definitions, margin bridge discipline, and working capital cycle transparency can matter more than headline revenue growth in restoring underwriting confidence.

Energy recoveries require capital structure clarity, capital investment discipline, and safety governance that investors believe will hold beyond the news cycle.

Governance episodes across sectors tend to resolve when investors can see who holds the decision levers for capital deployment, what constraints govern those levers, and how adherence will be reported.

The architecture is the same. The levers vary by industry and business model.

9.2. How to tell if a recovery is underway prior to quarterly reporting

You do not have to wait for reported numbers to assess whether the market is learning. There are four indicators to check routinely.

First, look at the scatter of analyst estimates and the shape of the tails. If the tails tighten and the median remains dense, your teaching objective is landing.

Second, track the language in notes and models. The test is whether the variables you emphasized become the variables analysts lead with.

Third, examine shareholder register quality. If turnover declines and the weight of long-horizon mandates increases, targeting is working.

Fourth, compare the relative movement of credit and equity. If credit spreads tighten while equity hesitates, lenders are assigning less default and governance risk, even if equity is still debating the growth and valuation path. Over time, equity often follows as uncertainty decays.

9.2.1. What breaks recovery and how to avoid it.

Three behaviors reset the clock. The first is changing your definitions mid-recovery. The market sees this as an effort to manage optics, and it widens the principal uncertainty margin. The second is guiding to a number that is outside your credibility curve. You may hit it, but if you, as an architect, miss timing, it will cost you two years of trust in an instant. The third is stuffing the story with metrics that cannot be reconciled to cash. You may feel more transparent, but you are teaching an analyst to tune you out.

The way around these traps is a pre-mortem before each earnings cycle. You list the two choices in your disclosure that could be mischaracterized, the one number that you cannot miss because it will dominate the lay narrative, and the one governance question that you will address in plain words. You make those answers part of your script, and you remove the adjectives.

9.2.2. Practitioner Conclusion:

Recovery is not a speech; it is a system. The market does not require perfection. The market requires a credible path that it can model without guesswork. When you choose the right drivers, reconcile them to GAAP, stagger proof through a visible ladder, and align your register with trusted mandates through volatility, valuation will begin to stabilize before operation is fully repaired. The cost of equity decreases as the uncertainty margins narrow. The cost of debt decreases as legal risk and governance risk are assessable and mitigated. The brand of management increases in the view of shareholders, as it can deliver inside the credibility curve versus promise outside of it.

The Chipotle experience showed the effectiveness of cadence and parsimony in a consumer brand recovery. The Unilever experience demonstrated that governance credibility can be established by changing the person accountable and clarifying how decisions are conveyed. The BP experience highlighted the value of concurrent architecture across the balance sheet, legal issues, and safety, which eliminated separate uncertainty premiums.

The work is similar across sectors: you reduce uncertainty by building systems that investors can test and trust. When that occurs, the market prices credibility, which is another way of saying it lowers your cost of capital.

Part III.
Transactions and Special Situations

Chapter 10.
IPOs, SPACs, and Listings

10.1. Introduction: transactions as valuation architecture

An initial public offering, cross-listing, direct listing, or de-SPAC is not a milestone. It is the point where a company essentially instructs some strangers on how to price the company's equity. The market does not buy adjectives. The market buys reconciled numbers, governance it can trust, and a cadence that establishes the future before it is identified. Entry terms are sticky because they embed personal credibility into the cost of capital. A rigorous entry reduces the equity risk premium and compounds through debt spreads, resale offerings, and acquisition currency. A promotional or early entry establishes a discount that can take years to hedge.

Transactions are pedagogy under maximum scrutiny. The company converts narrative into an executable model. It is a function of readiness, disclosures, orchestrating intermediaries, order book construction, and an aftermarket operating that reinforces the same vectors for the next four quarters. Anything less creates dispersion, volatility, and a permanent credibility tax.

10.2. Conceptual frame: Why entry terms persist

Entry establishes comparability, research vernacular, and marginal buyer. These are not readily rearranged. Multiples at listing become the anchor point for the sell-side target process. Ownership mix at listing sets market liquidity depth and velocity for many quarters. If analysts do not absorb the company's tenable variance at entry, they will rely on proxy heuristics. That increases dispersion and elevates the discount rate. If the register leans towards fast-money mandates, the incremental print in volatility will be determined by sellers who want to sell first and ask questions later. This is why the first forty-five days are more significant than nearly any other time period in a company's public life.

10.3. Preparedness and timing: audit that matters

Preparedness isn't revenue scale or momentum in a vacuum. It is sustaining public-market discipline without improvisation. A real audit starts twelve to eighteen months prior to filing. It puts four dimensions to the test.

Financial architecture asks if revenue recognition, margin structure, and cash conversion are explained reasonably clearly in accordance with GAAP or IFRS. If internal KPIs do not match the audited statements, the company is not prepared. This is where ASC 606, segment reporting, and policies for inventory or contract cost capitalization have to be final, not evolving.

Disclosure maturity asks whether the company has already taught the five or so operating variables that contribute to free cash flow variability. SaaS issuers must already show churn, cohort retention, unit economics, and payback with consistent definitions. Retailers must have already shown traffic, ticket, and mix, with gross margin as a core metric. Utilities must have already linked rate base growth and allowed returns to earnings. If the prospectus introduces new KPIs from scratch, skepticism rises, and analysts are forced to speculate.

Governance credibility asks if the board composition, committee independence, and incentive structure will pass institutional screens. A dual-class structure can be justified if it has sunset provisions and a clear policy rationale. Justifying controlled company exemptions only works with credible oversight and risk management. Internal control readiness (Section 404) needs to be materially feasible, not hope.

Strategic sequencing governs whether the company is telling the story investors want to hear at its stage of development. Pre-funding and early-stage companies must demonstrate proof of unit economics before they launch into the total addressable market. Mid-stage companies need to show the pathway to scale that does not deteriorate cash flow. Mature companies need to document capital returns and durability. There is a penalty for poor sequencing every time.

The contrast between Lyft and Spotify is a useful readiness lesson. Lyft came to market with heavy emphasis on bookings and market share, while key questions on unit economics and governance remained central for many investors. Spotify waited until market participants had a clearer framework for modeling gross margins, subscribers, churn, and ARPU. The direct listing benefited from that modelability. The point is not the transaction structure. It is that pedagogy has to be complete before you ask the public markets to underwrite duration.

10.4. Rules-based regulatory architecture frames the credibility of a company.

Legal and accounting frameworks do not substitute for credibility. They set the permitted boundaries of disclosure, and they determine which adjustments are acceptable, which are suspect, and which create liability.

JOBS Act and Emerging Growth Company status

EGC status can allow confidential submission and staged disclosure. Used properly, it gives management time to iterate through SEC comment cycles and tighten KPI definitions, reconciliations, and control readiness before the market is asked to underwrite the story in real time. Used poorly, it compresses the timeline and forces late-stage improvisation on non-GAAP definitions and guidance, which is when credibility breaks.

Regulation S K and Regulation S X

These rules shape the filing, including MD&A, segment reporting, and financial statement presentation. An MD&A that explains cause and effect in revenue, margin, and cash movement builds trust because it teaches the model. An MD&A that repeats marketing language invites harder SEC questions and leaves investors to infer mechanics on their own, which typically shows up as skepticism and dispersion.

Non-GAAP under Regulation G and Item 10(e)

Non-GAAP measures are permitted when they are clearly described, reconciled, and consistently defined. When definitions drift, or when adjustments appear designed to erase recurring economics, investors price the metric as noise rather than signal. The point is not to ban non-GAAP. The point is to make it auditable and repeatable.

Diligence, discipline, and Section 11 exposure

The defense is not rhetoric. It is a record. Audit committee oversight, a functioning disclosure committee cadence, documented review of sensitive disclosures, and a disciplined diligence process reduce both liability risk and credibility risk. Sloppy risk factor drafting increases litigation exposure and also undermines institutional confidence, particularly with investors who run internal legal review.

Sarbanes-Oxley and ICFR realism

Internal control assertions must match reality. If ICFR is weak, state it plainly, define the scope, and publish a remediation timeline with milestones. Claiming strong controls while remediating gaps is one of the fastest ways to lose trust with long-only investors who depend on stable definitions and repeatable numbers.

10.5. Building the prospectus: teach the model, not the dream

The prospectus is a curriculum design. It should validate the three to five operating drivers that explain most of the variability in free cash flow, and then reconcile each to the audited results.

For a software platform, this usually includes new cohort acquisition, expansion within cohorts, churn, and segment gross margin. It also requires explicit bridges from billings and deferred revenue to recognized revenue. For an asset-heavy industrial, it is capacity, utilization, pricing, and mix, input cost pass-through, maintenance versus growth capex, and the working capital mechanics that govern cash conversion. For a consumer brand, it is distribution reach, velocity, trade spend, and contribution margin by channel.

Risk factors should quantify ranges of outcomes and the levers that mitigate them, rather than repeat boilerplate. If there is a VIE structure, filings should name it plainly and outline the practical limits of enforcement. If customer concentration is material, disclose concentration levels and renewal dynamics. If a regulatory regime is changing, present scenarios rather than hoping reviewers do not ask.

The goal is for analysts to come away with a skeletal model they can flesh out, not a brochure that cannot be underwritten.

10.6. Orchestrating the intermediaries: incentives, conflicts, alignment

Bankers are focused on maximizing proceeds within a range of tolerable aftermarket performance. Underwriters want evidence of healthy demand and an orderly first-day trade that supports the book without creating an underpricing narrative. Auditors want a defensible perimeter around accounting judgments and adjustments. Counsel wants a defensible perimeter around liability and confidence that disclosures can withstand scrutiny. Exchanges, listing standards, and the SEC shape timing, structure, and process constraints. Investor relations and communications translate all of this into consistent language at every touchpoint.

The advisor's discipline is aligned with the selected drivers and the timing of evidence. If bankers start selling an earnings per share story in the filing that the business cannot support, stop it. If counsel pushes risk language that becomes so vague it cannot be explained plainly to institutions, tighten it until it is precise and usable. If the audit partner flags a non-GAAP add back that will not survive scrutiny, remove it before filing, not during the comment cycle. If governance fixes are expected for listing readiness, do not defer them to the week before pricing.

Alignment is not a slogan. It is daily work, and it is the difference between a coherent underwriting and a mixed message that gets priced as risk.

10.7. The U.S. IPO as pedagogy: S-1 to roadshow to allocation

The filing builds the syllabus. SEC review tests whether it is coherent. The roadshow runs the class and proves whether the lesson is landing. The order book and allocation determine who will carry the framework forward, and who will trade against it.

The roadshow is not a theater production. It is a sequence of teach-ins where the CFO and operating leaders answer the same ten questions the same way, repeatedly, until the market can model the company without interpretive guesswork. What drives gross margin? What drives churn? What governs sales efficiency over time? How price and mix will shift. How will reinvestment be financed? The best teams carry a one-page reconciliation sheet, write the drivers on the whiteboard in front of the investor, and force the discussion back to those variables.

The order book is often misread. Coverage ratios are secondary when the composition is wrong. A book that is multiple times covered by fast money is weaker than a tighter book anchored by long-only growth and core mandate accounts that can hold through volatility. The desk should be able to report a real-time view of order quality, price sensitivity, and demand by investor type. Allocation should favor aligned mandates and avoid rewarding accounts that are likely to flip on the opening print.

Price is not about extracting the last dollar. Price is where the stock can build a foundation. Overreaching into a fragile book invites a day two gap down, and that becomes the headline that frames the launch. A slightly more conservative price with the right owners can create more long-term value than a higher price that places stock in the wrong hands.

Stabilization matters. The greenshoe, syndicate short positions, and related aftermarket practices exist to reduce mechanical dislocation and disorderly trading. They cannot repair a flawed disclosure architecture, but they can prevent technical volatility from becoming a reputational event.

The quiet period and research initiation matter as well. Coverage is thinner than it used to be, and for many mid-cap issuers, there are fewer analysts doing deep work at launch. If the company has not taught a modelable framework through disclosure and the roadshow, early research can become commentary rather than a durable modeling anchor. In the first ninety days, that distinction matters because many portfolio decisions are driven by a small number of early notes that set the initial consensus frame.

10.8. Cross-border listing: harmonization of disclosure, translation of governance, liquidity layering

When discussing cross-border listings, three additional risks deserve explicit treatment: accounting comparability, governance translation, and liquidity fragmentation.

Accounting comparability is not solved by saying IFRS is close enough. Investors need a simple, repeatable map that shows how the issuer's reporting framework translates into the few lines that drive valuation under U.S. models. The goal is not to drown the reader in technical reconciliation. It is to give them stable bridges they can remember and reuse.

Governance translation is equally practical. U.S. institutions price governance risk in a familiar vocabulary: related party exposure, control rights, board independence, audit oversight, and enforceability. If the home market allows structures that U.S. investors tend to view as higher risk, the answer is not to minimize them. Name them plainly, explain the rationale, and show the oversight mechanisms that constrain abuse. The market can tolerate an unfamiliar structure more easily than it can tolerate ambiguity.

Liquidity fragmentation is the third risk. Cross-listed securities can suffer from split trading, inconsistent price discovery, and a free float that is thinner than it appears. A credible listing design makes price discovery explicit and creates a clear center of gravity for trading, so spreads, depth, and investor access reinforce rather than dilute one another.

Examples can help, but they should be used as illustrations rather than verdicts. Some cross-border issuers experienced periods where high cash burn and governance questions coexisted with active trading and elevated volatility, creating room for short sellers to frame the narrative. In those situations, stability tends to improve when the company discloses a small set of operational metrics with enough consistency that investors can underwrite progress quarter to quarter. Other issuers approached U.S. listings with governance and disclosure already aligned to institutional expectations, and the benefit was reflected in deeper liquidity and, in some cases, a lower cost of capital.

ADR mechanics should not be buried. Depositary structure, fees, and voting limitations affect certain funds' ability and willingness to own. If the listing uses a holding company structure or a VIE structure in jurisdictions where operating assets cannot be directly owned, state the ownership chain plainly. Clarify what U.S. investors legally own, what rights are contractual rather than equity rights, and what that implies for voting, cash flows, and enforcement. Describe the limits without promising comfort.

10.9. Direct listings: When they work and why

A direct listing replaces underwritten price discovery with an opening auction and a reference price. It works when the market already knows how to value the company, there is an existing base of informed holders who will sell in an orderly way over time, and management has already trained analysts to replicate the driver stack. It works less well when investors are asked to learn the valuation framework in real time, and early trading becomes the mechanism for discovery.

Spotify illustrates the favorable setup. In the years before listing, the company had effectively run a rolling education cycle. Subscriber economics, churn dynamics, ARPU, and margin structure were taught with enough consistency that many investors arrived with a model rather than a narrative. Companies that attempt the structure without the education can see erratic early trading and months of narrative noise that take quarters to unwind.

SPACs and de SPACs: structure without pedagogy

SPACs raise cash into a trust that public shareholders can redeem. Sponsors typically receive promotional economics that create dilution, and deal certainty often changes materially when redemption levels rise. Targets have historically leaned on forward projections and marketing style narratives that would face more friction in a traditional IPO context. PIPE financings are frequently used to backstop redemptions, but their signaling value depends on who the investors are, what the terms imply, and whether the capital is aligned with a long-horizon underwriting.

In the 2020 and 2021 wave, many de SPACs arrived in the public markets with limited readiness. The common pattern was elevated redemptions, fragile or highly structured PIPE arrangements, and rapid post-close volatility as the market repriced the gap between projections and proof.

Successful de SPACs impose IPO like discipline on themselves. The more credible examples tend to disclose unit economics with enough specificity to be modeled, keep definitions stable, and align the PIPE investor base with the underwriting horizon. In those cases, analysts adopt the driver stack, liquidity holds, and valuation is less dependent on sentiment.

Failed de SPACs tend to share three markers. Projections that outpace unit-level evidence. PIPEs structured with steep discounts and fast exit dynamics. Governance that reads like a private company even after a public listing.

One more layer now matters. The regulatory and litigation environment has tightened. Projection use and disclosure rigor in de SPAC transactions faces more scrutiny than it did in the peak cycle, and risk is less easily deflected by assuming broad safe harbor protection. The practical implication is straightforward: treat de SPAC execution like an IPO, and assume additional litigation sensitivity rather than viewing the structure as a shortcut.

If a sponsor forces a deal through with very high redemptions, waived minimum cash conditions, and an insider-heavy PIPE, the shell may still list, but the equity can trade like distressed equity-linked financing. The cost of the capital penalty will overwhelm the strategic rationale.

10.10. Order book microstructure: how supply composition drives volatility

Most management teams never understand how their order book was formed. They understand coverage ratios and a blended price sensitivity curve. They rarely, if ever, understand the split by mandate, turnover history, and factor style. This blindness is expensive. Order books dominated by momentum and market-neutral funds can produce clean prints and then disappear. Order books underpinned by core growth and quality funds can produce a boring open, but build a longer-term base.

A strong desk should provide history on flip rates by account, average post-deal holding periods, and factor correlations in drawdowns. With that information, allocation becomes a design decision. Anchors and cornerstones in certain markets are used to signal conviction. Clawback mechanisms are anticipated in the retail tranche in parts of Asia. Penalty bids and stabilization should be planned as insurance, not as a default posture.

There is a second layer of microstructure. Free float and lockup releases shape supply. If the company permits early releases for employees or early investors, the share count and the exact dates should be modeled against expected demand. An avoidable air pocket that creates a 10 percent gap down will be read as an execution failure, not bad luck.

10.11. After-market operating performance: the first 4 quarters set the multiple

Most IPO groups disband after the bell. This is a mistake. The first year is where credibility compounds or decays.

The first quarter should restate the driver stack almost verbatim. Definitions must match. Guidance must sit inside the credibility curve. If there is a miss, the explanation has to reconcile back to the drivers, not disappear into vague macro or one-off excuses. By the second quarter, analysts should be leading with the same variables you taught, or with clearly defined second-order drivers that are consistent with the original stack. If the drivers shift without a disciplined rationale, the company has lost the architecture. The third quarter is the natural investor day window for a deeper teach-in, assuming two quarters of consistent execution. The fourth quarter is where management has earned the option to expand ambition, or to reaffirm conservatism with credibility intact.

By this point, the system should operate as a closed loop. A perception study tests whether the driver's language has actually lodged. Ownership analysis tests whether turnover is declining in the mandate accounts you want, and rising only in the accounts that were never meant to be long-term owners. If misalignment remains, targeting has to change, and the content has to tighten.

The end of the quiet period and research initiation should not be left to chance. If teaching has worked, initiation notes should echo the architecture, not invent a new story.

Reg FD discipline does not bend. Selective disclosure to hand-picked funds eventually surfaces, and the credibility fallout is far too costly relative to any short-term benefit.

10.11.1. Case Study: Alibaba 2014

Alibaba sought access to the deepest global liquidity pool while carrying governance and structural features that many U.S. institutional investors routinely treat as higher risk. The VIE structure and the partnership model were not hidden risks. The test was whether the operating model could be disclosed in a way that investors could underwrite without relying on goodwill.

Disclosure Architecture

The filing described the legal structure plainly, rather than attempting to obscure it. The emphasis then shifted to the cash-generating mechanics investors could model: GMV, monetization, and take rate dynamics, and the translation from marketplace activity into revenue and margin. The workhorse of the narrative was not a promise. It was a set of repeatable operating bridges.

Book, Build, and Syndicate

Market commentary at the time emphasized broad demand and a book that could support multiple outcomes on pricing. The more important design question was not coverage statistics. It was aftermarket stability, which tends to be helped when allocations skew toward longer-horizon mandates rather than pure trading interest.

Aftermarket and Takeaways

Governance risk did not disappear, but it did not fully dominate the valuation frame in early coverage, because the operating model was legible. The takeaway is that transparent reconciliation can partially offset structural discomfort when the register is built around measurability and a longer horizon.

10.11.2. Case Study: Spotify 2018

Spotify chose a direct listing, which removed the familiar benefit of underwritten price discovery and the dampening effect that can come from traditional allocation control. That choice works best when investors arrive with models, not questions.

Disclosure Architecture

In the years prior, the company resourced an education process that made subscriber economics easier to model: adds, churn, ARPU, and gross margin, with stable definitions and consistent discussion of operating leverage rather than near-term profitability claims.

Pricing and Liquidity

A reference price and opening auction can function when both the buy side and sell side already share a valuation grammar. In that environment, the early days do not require the market to invent a framework through trading behavior.

Aftermarket and Lessons

The lesson is that a direct listing is not a shortcut. It is a structural choice that assumes teaching has already happened. The structure cannot substitute for pedagogy.

10.11.3. Case Study: Uber 2019

Uber came public with the visibility and scale of a private market emblem, but also with losses, regulatory exposure, and unresolved questions about unit economics across businesses. The IPO tested whether scale alone could carry valuation through skepticism.

Disclosure Architecture

The materials emphasized market scope and growth, but early investor debate often centered on the bounded economics: contribution margins, cohort behavior, and the path from scale to durable profitability. Where those bridges are not explicit, institutions tend to price a wider range of outcomes.

Order Book and Allocation

Pricing outcomes and early positioning reflected a market balancing enthusiasm against uncertainty. When allocations skew toward shorter-horizon holders, the stock can become a venue for debate rather than a platform for compounding ownership.

Aftermarket and Learnings

The early period was volatile, and valuation framing remained contested. The broader lesson is that scale is not a substitute for unit economics that are defined, reconciled, and repeated. If the register is not aligned with the path the company needs to travel, volatility becomes structural.

10.11.4. Case Study: DraftKings de SPAC 2020

The de SPAC cycle attracted speculative capital and elevated expectations. DraftKings is often cited as a case where investor education and unit economics disclosure were treated more like IPO discipline than promotional forecasting.

Disclosure Architecture

The narrative leaned on modelable drivers: customer acquisition economics, retention behavior, and product-level margin dynamics, with an effort to explain how spending linked to growth and how growth could translate into cash outcomes over time.

PIPE and Allocation

The signaling value of a PIPE is not the existence of the PIPE. It is the quality and horizon of the capital and the implied price sensitivity of the terms. De SPACs that anchor the structure in longer-horizon holders tend to face less immediate churn.

Aftermarket and Learnings

The takeaway is that format does not rescue weak disclosure, and format does not prevent strong disclosure from working. IPO discipline is still the stable play when markets are skeptical.

10.11.5. Case Study: Grab de SPAC 2021

Grab pursued a large platform valuation at a time when de SPAC fatigue was already visible. The central question was whether ambition was matched by a proof ladder and a clear bridge to cash.

Disclosure Architecture

Where filings lean heavily on TAM and platform aspiration without a compact unit economics bridge, the market tends to widen the range of valuation outcomes and compress the multiple to compensate for uncertainty.

Redemptions and PIPE

High redemptions and weak signaling from incremental capital often reinforce the perception that demand is price sensitive rather than conviction-based. That dynamic can leave the post close register fragile.

Aftermarket and Lessons

The common lesson is not that ambition is wrong. It is that ambition without a proof ladder is priced as risk, particularly when capital is no longer abundant.

10.11.6. Case Study: WeWork 2019

WeWork attempted to sell culture and community as economic defensibility, while governance and related party concerns were visible early. The market reaction illustrated a boundary condition for narrative.

Disclosure Architecture

Reliance on heavily adjusted metrics, weak reconciliation to sustainable cash generation, and governance issues that triggered institutional screens created a credibility problem that qualitative framing could not solve.

Outcome and Lessons

The transaction did not proceed as initially expected, and the valuation reset sharply. The lesson is that there are limits to storytelling. Without credible governance and modelable economics, public markets will not finance the gap between aspiration and proof.

10.12. Advisor's methods: the work products that drive outcomes

A serious capital markets advisor doesn't deliver slogans. The work is a suite of artifacts and cadences that produce the right interactions. A driver map detailing which three to five operating variables drive most variation in free cash flow. A reconciliation sheet linking the driver to GAAP. A disclosure definitions book that has locked wording so that it doesn't shift after the listing. An analyst training plan including the order of teach-ins, the ten hardest questions, and the model tabs that must be copied.

An allocation memo that ranks accounts based on mandate fit, turnover history, and sensitivity to factors, and tells the desk who should cover and who gets limited or no fills. An aftermarket calendar detailing the first four quarters: timing, metrics, philosophy of forecasting, perception studies, and a rule that definitions will remain constant even when the quarter is noisy. A governance memo that establishes, with respect to board and committee positioning, compensation alignment, and a dual-class sunset or controlled company messaging plan.

These artifacts are not optional. They are the only evidence, inside the company, that the transaction is being treated as pedagogy, not spectacle.

10.13. Synthesis: architecture vs. format

Format does not make or break a company. IPO, direct listing, cross listing, or de-SPAC all succeed when companies enter with readiness, reconciliation, aligned intermediaries, disciplined allocations, and an aftermarket operating system that recycles evidence until the market has institutionalized the model. They all fail when executives outsource pedagogy to the bookrunner, filings teach nothing of value to the model, allocations induce flip risk, and the first four quarters are treated as a victory lap rather than the actual class.

The market does not want perfection. It demands architecture. Companies that provide it earn a **valuation premium and a lower cost of capital**, which makes every strategic decision easier. Companies that do not will spend the next years paying a premium for credibility that marketing will not be able to offset.

Chapter 11.
M&A and Capital Events Deals

M&A and capital events are both the most visible and impactful inflection points for a company. They transform industries, adjust balance sheets, and reframe the way investors project long-term value. For capital markets advisors, these events are not just transactions; they are tests of credibility. The strategic rationale, disclosure discipline, financing structure, and integration process will determine if a deal expands valuation or destroys it. Similarly, capital events like buybacks, dividends, and recapitalizations are communicative signals of management's approach to shareholder returns. Collectively, these moments demonstrate the consistency or inconsistency between narrative and market trust.

The market does not price a transaction on the announced synergies or pro forma financials. It prices credibility. Credibility is established when companies sequence deals in time-disciplined increments, articulate rationale in ways investors can model, raise capital on terms that match their thesis, and provide the integration success that backs up their assumptions. Credibility is damaged when companies overpay, overpromise, or do not exhibit post-transaction discipline. This chapter will walk through the architecture of credibility in M&A and capital events, the mechanics that advisors use, and the lessons learned from successes and failures with notoriety.

11.1. Strategic Rationale and Credibility Architecture

All of this starts with a stated rationale. Management claims that a merger will achieve scale, obtain cost synergies, or enter new markets. Investors have become skeptical of these claims because the category has a long record of underdelivery. For an advisor, the challenge is not to restate the rationale, but to prove its credibility in the language of the model. Strategic rationale is credible if it ties directly to modelable drivers of cash flow. Cost synergies must be tied to specific line items in the P&L, with timing, run rate, and execution ownership. Revenue synergies must be grounded in observable overlap, contracted pathways, or demonstrated cross-sell behavior. Market extension must be matched with regulatory approval, distribution capabilities, and a plan for integration rather than a slide. Absent that linkage, the synergy rationale is interpreted as marketing and discounted in valuation.

The AOL–Time Warner merger is the poster child for a narrative-led rationale that could not be reconciled to cash. It was announced as a merger of old media and new technology, and touted as transformative. The market never received a credible bridge from concept to cash generation. Integration weakened, cultural gaps widened, and investors concluded the thesis was more imaginative than modelable. The deal destroyed shareholder value and remains a cautionary tale of storytelling without architecture.

In contrast, the 2006 Disney acquisition of Pixar was not framed in vague claims of innovation. It rested on complementary assets that investors could underwrite: Disney's distribution and franchise monetization machine, and Pixar's creative engine and track record. The disclosure linked the logic to box office performance, consumer products, licensing, and repeatable franchise economics. Integration was managed with discipline, including a clear approach to preserving Pixar's creative leadership. Investors could model the deal through established cash drivers, and the market rewarded the credibility of the architecture.

11.2. Readiness and Sequencing

Deals are won and lost before the transaction is made public. Readiness is the invisible architecture that determines whether the market will support a deal. A company needs to have built credibility over time, demonstrated delivery against guidance, and established a narrative in which the transaction reads as a logical next step, not a sudden reinvention.

Timing and sequencing matter because the market will not make a credibility leap without earned context. Kraft Heinz's approach to Unilever in 2017 illustrates the point. Kraft Heinz's equity story at the time was dominated by productivity and cost-cutting, with limited evidence of durable organic growth. That positioning did not create a credible bridge to buying a global, brand-led consumer platform at scale. The market reacted poorly, Unilever rejected the approach, and Kraft Heinz absorbed a credibility **hit** because the move read as reach rather than inevitability.

In contrast, Dell's acquisition of EMC in 2016 is a cleaner example of disciplined sequencing. Dell had already repositioned toward enterprise infrastructure and had established credibility in operating and financing complexity. EMC brought scale, strategic assets, and a value layer through its VMware stake, but the logic was presented as the next chapter in a storyline investors could already underwrite. The disclosures emphasized sources of cash flow, leverage, and deleveraging intent, financing mix, and integration priorities in terms that could be modeled. That sequencing turned a large transaction into a readable step, not a referendum on faith.

11.3. Disclosure & communication in M&A

M&A transactions are priced in the language of disclosure. Investors do not reward ambition in a press release. They underwrite filings, reconciliations, and the repeatable evidence that makes a pro forma story usable. Advisors earn their keep by making that disclosure system tight enough for institutions to model, challenge, and then trust.

Principle 1: Reconciliation. Pro forma narratives only become credible when they reconcile to GAAP or IFRS with clear bridges. Investors need to see how revenue, margins, cash conversion, and leverage translate from historical financials into a combined company model, with the adjustments labeled, bounded, and repeatable.

Principle 2: Consistent drivers. The few variables that matter must be disclosed the same way every reporting period. Investors can tolerate uncertainty, but not drift. When definitions change or "adjusted" metrics become pliable, analysts stop modeling and start discounting.

Principle 3: Milestones, not speculation. A deal case should include a small set of disclosed milestones that can be tracked quarter by quarter. If synergy logic cannot be measured and audited over time, the market treats it as optional and prices it as risk.

When these disciplines are ignored, valuation goes into a penalty box. General Electric's mid-2010s period is a useful caution. Definitions drifted, segment clarity was inconsistent, and "adjusted" framing was perceived as flexible. The result was not simply skepticism. It was wider dispersion in models, higher event day volatility, and pressure across both equity multiples and credit risk assessments because investors could not reconcile reported performance to underlying economics.

By contrast, strong acquirers use disclosure to teach the market how the portfolio works. In Microsoft's cloud transition, acquisitions were framed around recurring revenue mechanics, margin trajectory, and cross-sell logic that analysts could carry into models. The lesson is not that acquisitions automatically create value. It is that value compounds when the company can disclose the drivers, reconcile them cleanly, and report progress without drift until the market has institutionalized the framework.

11.4. Financing Style and Market Perspective

Financing is not done in the back room. Financing is a valuation outcome. The mix of debt, equity, and hybrids is a market signal about management confidence, risk appetite, and dilution philosophy. It also determines whether the transaction can be held through a down cycle without forcing defensive actions. Markets apply a credibility test to capital structure. If leverage is stretched, promised synergies do not protect the price. They often amplify skepticism.

Kraft Heinz is a cautionary example of leverage as a credibility constraint. Aggressive debt capacity assumptions, paired with a consolidation narrative, increased sensitivity to execution risk and rating pressure. As leverage concerns rose, spread pressure and downgrade risk became part of the equity conversation. Cost of capital moved against the company, narrowing strategic flexibility and making incremental consolidation harder to justify on acceptable terms.

Apple's capital return program illustrates the opposite dynamic: financing as a credibility enhancer. Even with significant cash generation, Apple chose to access debt markets at attractive spreads to fund buybacks and dividends while maintaining balance sheet flexibility. The structure signaled discipline rather than dependence: an issuer confident enough to optimize its capital stack without compromising resilience. Investors treated the program as an extension of operating credibility. Spreads remained tight, and the equity narrative benefited from the clarity of capital allocation.

Advisors have two jobs in financing architecture. The first is technical: design a capital structure that the balance sheet can carry under realistic downside cases. The second is interpretive: understand what that structure signals to equity and credit investors. Equity financing can protect flexibility but introduces dilution and can read as cautious if the rationale is not modelable. Debt financing preserves ownership but can become a credibility tax if it reduces headroom and forces the market to price refinancing or covenant risk. The discipline is making sure the financing structure matches the trust structure, so the deal can be underwritten as durable rather than hoped for.

11.5. Integration as the Ultimate Credibility Test

But eventually, the market discounts words and models. It prices actions. Integration is the ultimate credibility test in M&A. The synergy logic articulated at the announcement has to show up in milestones, results, and behavior. Cultural fit has to be managed, not assumed. Governance has to be credible enough that investors believe the deal will be run for value creation rather than internal politics.

Many failed deals were not concept failures. They were integration failures. AOL–Time Warner, Daimler–Chrysler, and HP–Autonomy broke because post-close execution did not deliver the promised operating reality. In each case, management underestimated cultural dissonance, overestimated synergy timing or size, and failed to build a governance system that could force accountability when the story began to drift.

Successful integration does the opposite. Disney–Pixar, Disney–Marvel, and Facebook–Instagram preserved the value engine while adding the advantages of scale. They integrated through stewardship rather than absorption, protecting the creative or product culture while the acquirer supplied distribution, capital discipline, and operating infrastructure. Investors could see continuity in the core value drivers, and they re-rated the combined story accordingly.

For advisors, integration communication is not a cosmetic layer. It is part of execution. Investors should be told what milestones define success, how those milestones connect to GAAP outcomes, and what the realistic timeline is. A well-designed integration narrative does not promise perfection. It provides a map that lets the market measure progress, quarter after quarter, until the deal is no longer a thesis, but a track record.

11.6. Capital Returns and Shareholder Signals

M&A is not the **only** form of capital event. Share buybacks, dividends, and recapitalizations are, in effect, direct signals of management's philosophy. These capital events are priced, not solely for the cash returned, but for what the cash **return implies** about confidence, discipline, and opportunity cost.

Share buybacks are rewarded when **they** operate within the credibility **curve**. Apple's share buyback program was rewarded as it occurred with consistency, prudent financing, and was linked to durable cash generation. In contrast, companies that announce opportunistic buybacks after periods of downdrafts usually experience a marginal valuation response, as the market **reads the action** as defensive.

Dividends produce comparable signals. Stable and predictable dividends have the effect of lowering the cost of capital by drawing in income-oriented funds with long investment horizons. Unexpectedly switching them is priced as a risk. GE's dividend cuts when in decline were not punished for the cash but for what they revealed about **deeper** credibility erosion.

Recapitalizations like special dividends or LBOs can unlock value or destroy value. The threshold for that differential is whether the capital event is aligned with narrative architecture. If leverage is consistent with disciplined cash generation, spreads tighten, and multiples expand. If leverage breaches credibility, you see penalties imposed by the market.

11.7. Synthesis

M&A and capital events are the loudest expressions of corporate ambition. They are not footnotes. They either reinforce or break credibility. Strategic rationale must stem from modelable drivers. Sequencing must reflect the company's credibility curve. Disclosures must provide investors with a model for how outcomes are expected to translate into results. Financing must rely on discipline. Integration will demonstrate the proof. Capital returns must be consistent with philosophy.

The lesson shared across the cases is the same. Disney, Microsoft, Dell, and Apple show credibility compounding when transactions, capital events, and architecture are in sync. AOL–Time Warner, Kraft Heinz, and GE show penalties incurred when the narrative and execution deviate. The market prices not just the fundamentals of the deal, but the architecture of trust surrounding it.

For the advisor, it is clear. Transactions and capital events are not just announcements. They are the definitive credibility trial in capital markets. They determine whether a company attracts premium multiples, keeps the right owners, and is resilient through cycles. Mastery is framing these moments as architecture, not theatre.

Chapter 12.
Activism and Defense

Shareholder activism has become a defining feature of today's capital markets. It no longer shows up only as hostile takeovers or episodic campaigns. It is now a persistent form of pressure through which investors attempt to shape strategy, capital allocation, governance, and, increasingly, environmental and social positioning. Activists position themselves as alternative architects of credibility, offering a competing narrative for how value should be unlocked.

Activism is both a risk and an opportunity for issuers. It is a risk when management credibility erodes, and the activist gains control of the core narrative. It is an opportunity when management responds with disciplined governance, clearer disclosure architecture, and a credible operating plan that investors can model and underwrite. Activism is not resolved in the media. It is resolved in modeling, in proxy voting behavior, and ultimately in valuation. The central question is simple: do investors trust management's architecture, or do they adopt the activist's model?

12.1. Activists as Competing Architects of Credibility

Activism is not about dividends and board seats only. It is about who controls the architecture of narrative. The activist constructs an alternative management model and argues that value can be unlocked through capital returns, divestitures, operating resets, or strategic pivots. Management defends its choices with a competing claim: that long-term value compounds more effectively along the current path, provided execution remains disciplined and outcomes remain measurable.

Activists succeed when they persuade long-only institutions that their model is more credible than management's, meaning it is clearer, more auditable, and more likely to produce a defined outcome within an acceptable timeframe. Activists fail when management has already built sufficient disclosure discipline and governance credibility such that investors can underwrite the plan without needing a new steward. In practice, management and activists are competing to define which attributes should anchor valuation and which risks deserve a higher discount rate.

Most campaigns rely on three elements of a playbook: critique of disclosure, critique of governance, and critique of capital allocation. Activists argue that management is obscuring true performance, that the board is misaligned or insufficiently accountable, or that capital is being deployed in ways that dilute value. Each lever works when credibility is weak. Each lever is blunted when the company has a credible, high-discipline architecture: stable metric definitions; clean reconciliation to GAAP and cash flow; governance structures that constrain agency risk; and a capital allocation framework that can be tested quarter by quarter against stated milestones.

12.2. Activism Methods

Disclosure critique

Activists often accuse management of opaque or misleading reporting. They introduce their own adjusted metrics to redefine performance and redirect the market's attention to a different scorecard. This is most effective when management has allowed definition drift in non-GAAP measures, overused adjustments that appear recurring, or failed to reconcile operating drivers to GAAP revenue, cash flow, and leverage in a way analysts can replicate.

Governance critique

Boards are framed as complacent, entrenched, or misaligned with owners. The critique typically targets director independence, tenure, skill mix, oversight quality, and incentive design. Where executive compensation appears detached from shareholder outcomes, or where risk governance looks performative, activists can argue that weak accountability is the root cause of strategic underperformance and valuation discounting.

Capital allocation critique

Activists argue that cash is being stockpiled without purpose, that buybacks and dividends are mis-sized or mistimed, or that acquisitions destroy value through overpayment and integration risk. They position themselves as agents of discipline who will release trapped value through divestitures, recapitalizations, or a narrower operating focus.

These levers only convert into momentum when institutions conclude that management's architecture is weaker than the activist's, meaning less measurable, less credible, or less likely to deliver within a realistic horizon. When disclosure is consistent, boards are visibly engaged, and capital allocation is tied to auditable decision rules, activism struggles to gain traction because the market already has a workable model and an accountable governing system.

12.3. Defensive Architecture

Defending against activism is beyond tactics deployed when an activist emerges. It is a structure that must exist well before. The first element in that structure is disclosure. Companies consistently disclose the same results, disclose operational drivers in a way that reconciles to GAAP, and avoid the distraction of non-GAAP measures, which rob activists of a uniform entry point.

When activists try to replace reported results with their modified figures or suggest undisclosed shortfalls, they will have less traction if management has already established clarity that investors believe in.

Governance is the second layer. A Board that refreshes consistently, has transparency of composition, and has an obvious connection between executive pay and shareholder impact leaves little opportunity for critics to pierce. Activists flourish if they find entrenched board members or pay structures that reward management regardless of performance. When a company has already established its governance framework with shareholder input, it becomes hard work to convince investors that a new governance structure is needed.

Third is capital allocation. Activists often make the claim that companies mishandle their surplus cash by parking it, over-allocating to speculative investment opportunities, or doing dilutive acquisitions. Management that can articulate its capital allocation philosophy, weigh the merits of buybacks, dividends, reinvestment, and acquisitions, and consistently execute on them lowers that point of engagement. Investors are usually not swayed by an activist's narrative if they know and embrace management's capital allocation philosophy.

Finally, defense entails investor segmentation. In a proxy contest or contested situation, the pivotal votes often come not from hedge funds, but from long-only institutions with low turnover and large ownership positions. These long-only investors evaluate credibility based on long-term trust rather than short-term upheaval. Organizations that regularly engage these investors and educate them on disclosure architecture and governance discipline create resilience. If activists come to them, they will be predisposed to supporting management if management has established credibility.

The coupling of a disclosure system, governance differentiation, and capital allocation discipline tied to investor segmentation is the architecture of defense. These elements do not ensure that there will never be activists, but they assure that activists will have to work uphill to win the narrative.

12.4. Common Failure Modes

Defensive failures are rarely about a weak rebuttal memo. They are usually the predictable consequence of credibility gaps that were allowed to compound. The first failure mode is definition drift, where non-GAAP measures, segment disclosures, or "adjusted" narratives change often enough that investors stop treating reported results as a stable currency. The second is governance opacity, where board oversight, incentives, and accountability are not legible to institutional screens, making it easier for an activist to argue that agency risk is being ignored. The third is capital allocation inconsistency, where buybacks, dividends, reinvestment, and M&A appear reactive or contradictory, creating the impression that management is optimizing for discretion rather than shareholder value. The fourth is holder misalignment, where management has not built durable relationships with long-only decision makers, leaving the vote to be influenced by whoever frames the issue most simply at the moment of conflict.

When these conditions exist, activism becomes less a surprise attack and more the market's formal mechanism for renegotiating trust.

12.5. What Successful Defense Signals

A successful defense is usually visible in the company's operating cadence before any activist emerges. Investors observe stable definitions and explicit reconciliations that allow modeling discipline to persist through volatility. They observe governance accountability that is credible in structure, not merely stated, including refreshment, oversight clarity, and incentives that map to shareholder outcomes. They observe a capital allocation philosophy that has a hierarchy, a repeatable logic, and an execution record, reducing the plausibility of "trapped value" claims. They also observe a register where long-only holders are present, informed, and engaged, which changes the proxy math, because the pivotal voters already understand management's architecture and can test activist claims against it.

Defense succeeds when credibility is already institutionalized. It fails when management tries to manufacture trust at the same time it is being challenged.

12.6. Advisor's Toolkit for Activism Preparedness

Advisors preparing companies for activism follow a process similar to stress testing. The first step is an audit of disclosure, meaning you identify any reporting that could be interpreted as vague, inconsistent, or opaque. If operational drivers are reported without reconciliation, if adjustments are not consistent, or if guidance shifts unpredictably, you have created potential sites of activist criticism. The remedy is not more narrative. It is a tighter architecture: a smaller universe of decisive variables, explicit bridges to GAAP, stable definitions, and a disciplined cadence that teaches the market how to model the company.

The second step is an audit of governance. Advisors evaluate board composition against institutional expectations, including tenure, independence, skill coverage, and oversight credibility. They review incentive plans to verify that payouts map to shareholder outcomes rather than internal convenience metrics. Shortcomings are addressed through refreshment, skill matrices, incentive redesign, and clearer committee accountability. When these actions are done preemptively, management enters contested periods with credibility rather than defensiveness.

The third component is long-only engagement. Advisors segment the shareholder base to prioritize the investors most likely to determine the outcome of a contest. In practice, these are long-horizon institutions with process-driven voting. Advisors structure regular engagement that builds familiarity with the company's disclosure logic, governance posture, and capital allocation philosophy. Trust is the most reliable barrier against activist momentum.

Scenario planning is the next component. Advisors anticipate what activists will argue for, including higher buybacks, divestitures, governance changes, or a revised strategic posture. They build evidence-based responses that live in the investor's language: model logic, disclosure bridges, peer comparisons, and credible timelines. The objective is not rhetorical sparring. It ensures the company can answer pressure questions in a way that preserves architecture and prevents improvisation.

The final component is narrative alignment by mandate. Advisors assess whether the company's chosen path matches the investor mandates it is appealing to. If management is optimizing for reinvestment and growth, the register must contain investors who underwrite reinvestment. If the company is optimizing for return of capital, the story must be legible to capital return mandates. Misalignment creates a vacuum that activists can exploit. Alignment reduces the activist's available narrative space.

This toolkit is not designed for one-off use. It should be embedded into routine investor relations, governance disclosure, and capital allocation communications so that readiness becomes continuous rather than reactive.

12.7. Synthesis

Activism is not episodic. It is the market's mechanism for contesting credibility when confidence in management architecture weakens. Activists win when they can offer institutions a simpler, more auditable model of value creation than management has provided. Management wins when disclosure is stable and reconciled, governance is accountable and legible, capital allocation is coherent and executed, and the shareholder base is built around long-only mandates that prefer compounding over disruption.

The central lesson is that the struggle is not decided in the press. It is decided in the investor's model and the proxy voter's framework. Preparedness is therefore not a crisis response. It is an operating system. Companies that build it force activists to argue uphill. Companies that do not end up litigating credibility at the worst possible moment, when the register is unsettled, and the market is least forgiving.

Chapter 13.
Crisis and Litigation

Crisis and litigation are the sharpest shocks a public company can absorb. They can erase years of equity value in days, widen credit spreads overnight, and permanently alter how investors underwrite duration risk. These events often originate outside management's control, but the valuation outcome rarely turns on the incident alone. It turns on whether management can respond with credible disclosure, visible governance, and a verifiable path to resolution.

Markets price credibility. They penalize opacity, defensiveness, and minimization. They reward factual clarity, accountable oversight, and corrective action that can be tracked. For a capital markets advisor, a crisis is not a break in the investor system. It is the moment when that system is stress tested most severely.

13.1. Conceptual Framework: Crisis as a Credibility Stress Test

A crisis compresses years of credibility building into a narrow window of scrutiny. Investors must decide, quickly, whether to maintain trust in management's framework, reprice the issuer with a permanent risk premium, or exit entirely. Litigation compounds this dynamic by adding uncertainty about magnitude, timing, and governance exposure, all of which expand the error bands in models.

The core principle is that the market does not price the event mechanically. Two companies can face similarly severe incidents and experience radically different outcomes because credibility differs. A recall can be priced as a contained cost if disclosures are consistent, milestones are explicit, and governance is visibly engaged. The same recall can be priced as structural impairment if disclosures drift, oversight appears weak, or remediation remains ambiguous.

The advisor's role is not to eliminate crisis risk. It is to ensure that, if a crisis occurs, the issuer has an architecture capable of preserving investor trust while uncertainty is being resolved.

13.2. Timely Transparency

The first determinant of crisis valuation is the speed and completeness of disclosure. Markets penalize silence and delay because uncertainty is priced as risk. Early communications should acknowledge the incident, distinguish confirmed facts from open questions, and establish a disciplined cadence for updates.

This is not a public relations posture. It is financial communication. Credit and equity investors need a stable information regime to avoid compounding worst-case assumptions. Even when facts are incomplete, cadence and accountability reduce the premium investors demand.

13.3. Control of the Narrative

Crisis creates competing narratives. Media speculation, regulatory statements, political noise, and counterparties can all amplify uncertainty. If management does not establish a clear factual center, external voices define the framing and the market prices that frame.

Narrative control does not mean spin. It means disciplined repetition of what is known, what is being investigated, what will be updated and when, and which governance bodies are overseeing the response. Advisors help management avoid improvisation, prevent contradictory statements across channels, and keep forward-looking speculation from substituting for evidence.

13.4. Milestones of Resolution

Markets do not heal on adjectives. They heal on milestones. Credibility is restored when investors can track progress through observable steps, such as remediation completion, regulatory clearance, settlements, reserve establishment, claims frameworks, or operational safety improvements.

Milestones reduce uncertainty incrementally. Each confirmed milestone narrows model dispersion, tightens credit assumptions, and compresses the risk premium that was applied at the shock.

13.5. Failure Patterns in Crisis Management

13.5.1. BP and Deepwater Horizon (2010)

Deepwater Horizon is a modern reference point for how credibility can deteriorate during crisis response. Early communications were criticized for underestimating the scope and for revisions that appeared reactive rather than anchored in a stable disclosure process. The market response reflected a conclusion that uncertainty was not being bounded decisively. Equity repriced sharply, credit spreads widened, and the cost of capital carried a persistent premium relative to peers because the market treated the incident as both a liability event and a credibility event.

13.5.2. Volkswagen and Dieselgate (2015)

Dieselgate illustrates how governance framing can intensify valuation damage. Once regulators disclosed the emissions issue, the market's focus shifted quickly from unit economics to integrity, oversight, and exposure. Delayed accountability and unclear remediation sequencing contributed to prolonged uncertainty. Valuation damage reflected not only expected penalties and costs, but also an embedded governance premium that lingered beyond the initial financial estimates.

13.5.3. Wells Fargo and Unauthorized Accounts (2016)

The unauthorized accounts scandal demonstrates how cultural and incentive failures can become structural risk in investor models. The market treated the event less as an isolated compliance issue and more as evidence of governance weaknesses and misaligned incentives. Even as financial impacts were quantified, credibility erosion persisted because investors assumed the risk could recur in other forms.

13.6. Crisis Management Discipline

13.6.1. Johnson and Johnson and Tylenol (1982) and later litigation exposure

The Tylenol case remains a gold standard for decisive response. A rapid recall, clear public communication, and durable packaging changes created an observable corrective path. Markets tend to reward this posture because it compresses uncertainty and demonstrates governance command.

Later litigation exposure, including opioid related claims, shows a different challenge, long-duration legal uncertainty. In those contexts, disciplined loss contingency disclosure, settlement frameworks, and credible governance oversight can reduce volatility even when reputational damage persists. The lesson is not that markets ignore harm. The lesson is that markets react to price uncertainty more quickly when the liability perimeter and the governance response are made measurable.

13.6.2. Toyota and Recall Discipline (2010)

Toyota's recalls demonstrate how a crisis can evolve from valuation impairment to valuation recovery when disclosure and remediation become systematic. As transparency improved, collaboration with regulators became visible, and corrective actions were communicated in a trackable sequence; investors began to treat the event as containable. Multiples recovered as the market concluded that governance and process were regaining control.

13.7. Advisor's Toolkit for Crisis and Litigation Preparedness

Effective crisis response is built before the crisis occurs. The toolkit is structural:

Disclosure infrastructure: The company needs the internal ability to quantify operational disruption or legal exposure against GAAP and liquidity quickly, and to communicate that perimeter without improvisation.

Governance protocols and drills: Boards should have defined escalation paths, independent verification mechanisms, and clear oversight roles. Visible board engagement reduces agency risk precisely when investors are most sensitive to it.

Communication cadence templates: Pre-built templates help management communicate facts, uncertainty, actions, and timing consistently. This prevents contradictory messaging and reduces speculation premiums.

Financial preparedness: Companies should have pre-planned approaches to reserving, liquidity management, and funding remediation. Investors prefer early bounded estimates, with updates as facts evolve, over silence followed by a surprise.

Milestone mapping: Advisors help management identify the milestones investors will demand, then publish a credible timeline and report progress against it until uncertainty compresses.

13.8. Synthesis

Crises and litigation are not priced solely on operational damage or legal exposure. They are priced as credibility tests. Companies that delay, minimize, or allow disclosure drift invite a higher and often persistent cost of capital. Companies that communicate quickly, reconcile exposures to financial frameworks, activate visible governance oversight, and provide milestones of closure can stabilize valuation sooner, even when outcomes remain uncertain.

BP, Volkswagen, and Wells Fargo illustrate how governance and disclosure failures can turn an incident into a structural discount. Johnson and Johnson and Toyota illustrate how disciplined disclosure and remediation can reduce the uncertainty premium and support recovery.

For capital markets advisors, the conclusion is simple. Crisis is not a communications theater. It is credibility management under constraint. Preparedness is an operating system that integrates disclosure discipline, governance protocol, financial framing, and milestone-based resolution until the market has no reason to price additional surprise.

Chapter 14. Transformation, ESG, and Policy

Companies are no longer valued solely on near-term financial results. Investors now underwrite longer duration questions: whether a business model can be reinvented without destroying cash generation, whether sustainability claims are measurable and enforceable, and whether policy exposure is being managed as a financial risk rather than a reputational debate. Transformation, ESG, and policy are not separate themes. They are credibility systems. They influence the size of model error bands, the stability of multiples, and the cost of capital.

When managed with discipline, these systems compress uncertainty and attract long only capital. When treated as marketing, they widen dispersion, invite activism, and create permanent discounts.

14.1. Transformation as Infrastructure of Evidence

Corporate transformations are frequently announced and rarely underwritten. Investors do not price "reinvention" unless it is expressed as a sequence of interim states that can be measured, reconciled to financial statements, and governed with clear accountability.

The primary failure mode is narrative overhang: management asserts a multi-year transformation while disclosures do not provide evidence in the current period that the economics are changing. The market prices the gap between ambition and evidence as risk. That risk shows up as higher dispersion, a lower multiple, and a higher cost of capital.

Transformation becomes credible when disclosures follow a proof ladder. Early disclosures show unit economics and adoption mechanics. Mid-stage disclosures show scaling and margin structure. Later disclosures show resilience, cash conversion, and capital allocation discipline. The advisor's role is to design the sequencing, define metrics precisely, and ensure each metric bridges cleanly to GAAP outcomes so the street can model the transition without inventing its own assumptions.

14.1.1. Case: Microsoft Cloud Transition

Microsoft's transition from licensing to cloud services illustrates the credibility built through disclosure architecture. Management did not rely on labels. It trained investors to model recurring revenue dynamics, margin expansion through scale, and the durability of customer relationships. Over time, analysts learned how to reconcile these operating disclosures back to reported results and to reclassify the business in their models. The multiple expansion occurred alongside this learning curve because the market could underwrite the transition with a cleaner framework, not because the company claimed to be transformed.

14.1.2. Case: General Electric and Narrative Drift

General Electric illustrates the opposite pattern. Transformation claims were repeated while the disclosure set became more complex, definitions drifted, and performance was difficult to reconcile across segments and periods. When guidance credibility weakens, the market does not simply lower estimates. It raises the discount rate. The outcome is multiple compressions and a higher cost of capital, which then makes transformation harder to fund. The lesson is that transformation without stable definitions, reconciliation, and repeatable evidence does not create optionality. It consumes it.

14.2. ESG as an Architecture of Disclosure

ESG has moved from an optional narrative to an embedded mandate constraint for many investors. In practice, ESG affects valuation when it changes how investors model risk, resilience, and license to operate. It is not "priced" because a company publishes a sustainability report. It is priced when disclosures are useful, comparable, and linked to financial consequences.

The credibility failure mode is performative disclosure: glossy outputs that are not tied to operating outcomes, do not follow recognized frameworks, and cannot be verified. That is not neutral. It increases skepticism and often accelerates activist vulnerability.

ESG credibility requires three things: a defined framework, metrics that are measurable and consistent over time, and verification appropriate to the claim. The advisor's job is to prevent ESG from becoming a parallel narrative and instead make it part of the same disclosure discipline that governs financial reporting.

14.2.1. Case: Ørsted's Renewable Transition

Ørsted's transition is an example of ESG becoming economically modelable. The company disclosed transition progress in ways investors could reconcile with project economics and cash generation, and it supported credibility with external assurance. The market did not reward aspiration. It rewarded measurability, governance of execution, and evidence that the transition had a stable financial logic.

14.2.2. Case: ExxonMobil and ESG Fragility

ExxonMobil's experience around the Engine No. 1 campaign illustrates that ESG can become a governance and capital allocation credibility test. The vulnerability was not created by a single quarter's operating performance. It came from a perception gap between investor mandate evolution and the company's disclosure and governance posture. When the market believes a company is behind the mandate curve, it becomes easier for an activist to argue that the board and capital allocation discipline are misaligned with long-duration risk.

14.3. Policy Engagement is a Valuation Framework

Policy exposure is a financial variable. Regulation shapes addressable markets, cost structures, liability boundaries, and competitive dynamics. Investors are not asking whether a company has opinions. They are asking whether the company can operate predictably across regulatory regimes, and whether policy risk is being managed with discipline.

Policy engagement becomes a valuation positive when it reduces downside tails and improves planning certainty. It becomes a valuation negative when it signals governance risk, enforcement exposure, or an unstable license to operate. Advisors add value by translating policy into model terms: what changes the range of outcomes, what shortens or extends timing, and what alters cash conversion.

14.3.1. Case: Mexico's ESG Sovereign Bonds (2019)

Mexico's sustainable bond framework illustrates how policy architecture can change demand composition and pricing. A defined use of proceeds, a reporting cadence, and external review mechanisms broadened the buyer base and improved execution outcomes. The underlying macro fundamentals did not change in the short term. The pricing benefit reflected the credibility of the framework and the transparency of ongoing reporting.

14.3.2. Case: Big Tech Antitrust Proceedings

Large platform companies illustrate how policy risk can become an embedded valuation premium when disclosures do not provide investors with a bounded framework for the range of regulatory outcomes. When investors feel forced to guess the enforcement path, remedies, and timing, they widen error bands and apply a governance and policy discount. The lesson is not that regulation is uniquely punitive. It is that uncertainty, if left unstructured, that will be priced.

Advisor Toolkit for Transformation, ESG, and Policy. The advisor's toolkit is one integrated system.

The first element is milestone sequencing. Transformation claims are staged into measurable interim states that can be reconciled to financial statements and repeated with stable definitions.

The second element is ESG discipline. Disclosures are aligned to recognized frameworks, scoped to material metrics, and supported by verification that matches the strength of the claim. The goal is comparability and auditability, not volume.

The third element is policy framing. Regulatory exposure is translated into scenarios, timing ranges, and financial impacts, so investors can model the distribution rather than debate the narrative.

Together, these elements create credibility under long-duration uncertainty.

14.4. Synthesis

Transformation, ESG, and policy now sit inside valuation rather than beside it. Companies that treat them as marketing expand uncertainty, invite activist narratives, and earn a permanent discount. Companies that treat them as disclosure architecture compress uncertainty and earn a lower cost of capital.

The cases reinforce a single lesson. When transformation is sequenced into evidence, when ESG is made measurable and verifiable, and when policy exposure is framed as a modelable risk, credibility compounds. When definitions drift, disclosures become performative, or policy risk is left unbounded, the market raises the discount rate. For the capital markets advisor, the work is not persuasion. It is constructing the architecture that makes long-duration underwriting rational.

Part IV.
Sectors, Tools, Futures

Chapter 15.
Sector Patterns

Advising in the capital markets cannot assume that all businesses are priced the same way. A framework that persuades investors in pharmaceuticals may not translate to industrials. A disclosure practice that builds confidence in banking may be irrelevant in consumer markets. Narrative architecture is always situational.

Investors do not model "a company." They model a sector playbook, then test whether an issuer fits it. Each sector has a small set of variables that carry most explanatory weight for cash flow and risk. Credibility is judged relative to those variables, and relative to the disclosure norms investors already trust.

In this chapter, we review six sectors: healthcare, financials, energy, technology, consumer, and industrials. For each sector, we outline how valuation tends to be modeled, where credibility breaks first, and what patterns repeatedly distinguish resilient credibility from fragile narrative.

15.1. Healthcare: The Proof Economy

Healthcare is priced on proof. Investors demand clinical evidence, regulatory clarity, and a credible adoption pathway. Without those, even strong narratives struggle to clear the discount rate.

A frequent failure pattern is incomplete translation from scientific progress to modelable revenue. Biogen's Aduhelm illustrates how approval alone does not resolve the investor model when endpoints remain contested, and payer behavior is uncertain. The credibility gap is not only scientific. It is also a disclosure design, meaning the absence of a coherent framework for adoption, pricing, access, and persistence that investors can update with each milestone.

Vertex illustrates the opposite pattern. Disclosures tend to be legible to modeling: trial design, outcome interpretation, regulatory posture, and the commercial constraints that govern penetration and durability. Investors can build adoption curves with explicit assumptions, rather than guessing at what management means.

Advisor Role in Healthcare Advisors should design disclosure as a proof ladder: clinical evidence, regulatory pathway, payer access, and adoption cadence. Investors do not need certainty. They need a sequence of testable milestones that narrows uncertainty without changing definitions each quarter.

15.2. Financials: Durability as Premium

Financials are valued on durability. Investors focus on net interest margin, credit quality, loss provisioning, liquidity, and capital adequacy. They pay a premium when they believe a franchise can compound through stress and still protect capital.

JPMorgan illustrates durability as a premium. Conservative guidance, consistent reporting, and clear linkage between risk posture and capital metrics make the franchise easier to underwrite through cycles. That is what the market rewards.

Credit Suisse illustrates the opposite pattern: the erosion of trust when risk exposures and governance weaknesses are perceived as recurring, not episodic. When investors cannot reconcile disclosures with risk outcomes, equity and credit both price a governance premium long before an acute event forces repricing.

Advisor Role in Financials Advisors should anchor the narrative in resilience variables that investors already price: capital, liquidity, provisions, and risk concentration. Promotional guidance is less useful than disciplined, repeatable disclosure and a credible explanation of variance.

15.3. Energy: Transition and Trust

Energy remains exposed to commodity cycles, but credibility is increasingly tested through capital allocation discipline and transition governance. Investors want evidence that cash returns, balance sheet durability, and transition commitments are measurable and constrained by a decision framework.

Ørsted illustrates how transition credibility can be priced when the market can audit capital allocation logic and track outcomes against a stable structure. The market pays for measurable transition, not for slogans.

BP after Deepwater Horizon illustrates the persistence of a credibility discount when legal overhang, safety governance, and operational risk are not treated as a structured reporting system. A crisis is not only an event. It is a multi-quarter test of whether management can operate under scrutiny with consistency.

Advisor Role in Energy Advisors should help issuers separate three disclosure lanes and keep them consistent: capital allocation, operational risk and safety governance, and transition commitments with measurable reporting. The market discounts transition narratives that cannot be audited.

15.4. Technology: From Adjectives to Economics

Technology issuers often present disruption as identity. Investors price unit economics, retention, and operating leverage. The credibility test is whether growth is purchased or earned, and whether the path to cash generation is explainable without changing the story every quarter.

WeWork remains the cautionary reference: narrative strength cannot substitute for governance credibility and cash flow logic. When disclosures do not allow a model to be built, public markets treat aspiration as risk.

Microsoft illustrates the constructive pattern in a pivot. The market re-rates when disclosures consistently teach the variables that matter to the new economic model and reconcile them to GAAP in a stable way. Operational progress matters, but it scales into valuation only when the market's model updates.

Advisor Role in Technology Advisors must translate technical narratives into a small driver stack: retention, expansion, acquisition efficiency, and margin trajectory. The work is not to add metrics. It is to impose hierarchy, definitions, and reconciliation.

15.5. Consumer: Sentiment and Fundamentals

Consumer models rely on traffic, conversion, basket, pricing, and margin. But consumer valuation also carries sentiment risk, meaning investors demand confidence that the brand and customer behavior will hold under pressure.

Chipotle illustrates disciplined recovery via simplicity. Management anchored disclosure to a small set of drivers that investors can audit and reconcile, and repeated them long enough for the market to stop debating the category of outcome and start debating magnitude and timing.

Wells Fargo illustrates the durability of a trust penalty when misconduct changes the perceived reliability of internal controls and governance, even when the operating data later improves. In consumer adjacent franchises, trust is an input to the discount rate.

Advisor Role in Consumer Advisors should keep disclosure tight: the handful of operating variables that connect directly to cash generation, plus a credible account of what rebuilds trust when it has been impaired. Sentiment matters most when it is connected to measurable operating outcomes.

15.6. Holding Governance as Valuation for Industrials

Industrials are modeled through cycles. Investors watch backlog quality, utilization, pricing and mix, cost pass-through, working capital discipline, and cash conversion. A credibility premium is earned when capital allocation and reporting discipline reduce cycle uncertainty.

Caterpillar illustrates the value of disciplined cycle communication when investors can map backlog and demand signals into cash generation without narrative drift. When the market believes in the cycle framework and the cost discipline, it assigns a more stable multiple.

GE illustrates the long cost of drift: shifting definitions, inconsistent segment logic, and repeated credibility breaks widen dispersion and raise the required return. Remediation takes time because investors require consistent delivery, not revised language.

Siemens offers a contrasting pattern where disclosure consistency and portfolio logic enable investors to underwrite the business through cycle shifts with less uncertainty.

Advisor Role in Industrials Advisors should enforce disciplined disclosure around backlog, conversion, and capital allocation rules that remain stable through cycles. Promissory disclosures are punished. Repeatable reconciliation is rewarded.

15.7. Cross-Sector Comparisons

Cross-sector comparisons clarify why sector fluency matters. Healthcare and technology can both be growth narratives, but healthcare requires clinical substantiation while technology requires unit economics and retention proof. Financials and industrials both price durability, but financials are governed by capital and liquidity constraints, while industrials are governed by utilization, backlog, and cash conversion. Consumers and energy both face trust shocks, but consumer trust is behavioral while energy trust is institutional and governance-based.

The architecture is consistent across sectors: identify the few drivers that explain outcomes, define them, reconcile them to audited results, and repeat them until the market institutionalizes the model. What changes are the driver set and the credibility failure mode?

15.8. Synthesis

Credibility is context-specific. Each sector has a different model language, different disclosure norms, and different penalties for drift. Advisors add value by translating strategy into the language investors already price, then building a cadence that keeps definitions stable and evidence cumulative.

Chapter 16 shifts from sector translation to the advisor's toolbox: the research stacks, dashboards, and templates that make credibility reproducible rather than personality-driven.

Chapter 16.
Tools and Methods

Frameworks matter only if they can be repeated. A strong meeting can impress, but it rarely changes valuation by itself. Credibility must be instrumented, meaning it must be supported by systems that keep disclosures consistent, reconciled, and auditable across cycles.

Tools are not cosmetics. They are the internal evidence that a company is treating capital markets as an operating system, not as an occasional performance.

16.1. Research Stacks: Building Analytical Foundations

A research stack integrates primary disclosures, investor interpretation, and external signals into one disciplined process. The goal is not more data. The goal is fewer variables that explain most variance in cash flow and risk.

Core components include filings and audited results, earnings scripts and guidance history, analyst notes and model structures, peer disclosure norms, and governance and regulatory signals. Optional layers include alternative data only when it has a demonstrable bridge to financial outcomes. Perception work rounds out the stack by testing whether the intended driver language is being adopted or merely heard.

A research stack becomes useful only when it is synthesized into a small driver map and a clear set of disclosure decisions.

16.2. Dashboards: Educating Variance Drivers

Dashboards are not decorative. They are the mechanism that forces internal and external alignment around the drivers that matter.

A bank dashboard should make capital, liquidity, credit, and margin drivers visible and reconcilable. A consumer dashboard should emphasize traffic, basket, pricing, and margin with clear bridges. A software dashboard should emphasize retention, expansion, acquisition efficiency, and margin trajectory.

The implementation is the point. A dashboard works when the same driver structure appears in earnings remarks, Q&A, follow-ups, and subsequent quarters, without definition drift.

16.3. Templates: Create Disciplined Process

Templates convert episodic communication into a repeatable system. They prevent reinvention, reduce drift, and make credibility cumulative.

The earnings template should preserve a stable order: results and variance, driver reconciliation to GAAP, then guidance calibrated to the credibility curve. Investor day templates should tie strategy to modelable outcomes and avoid introducing new drivers that contradict the earnings architecture. Crisis templates should separate operational, financial, and governance lanes and enforce cadence even when information is constrained.

Templates exist to restrain overreach, prevent secrecy, and keep definitions stable under pressure.

16.4. Integration: Tools as Architecture

Research stacks identify the drivers that matter. Dashboards expose them. Templates force them to be repeated with discipline. Together, they create a closed loop system: diagnose, disclose, teach, audit adoption, then refine.

When applied consistently, these tools reduce dispersion, improve mandate alignment, and lower the premium investors demand for uncertainty. They make credibility something the organization can produce, not something it hopes to be granted.

16.5. Synthesis

Credibility becomes durable when it is reproducible. Research stacks provide analytical clarity, dashboards establish the model language, and templates enforce cadence and consistency across cycles. Without this structure, the capital markets strategy remains fragile. With it, valuation becomes more stable, the cost of capital improves, and strategic choices become easier to finance.

If you want, I can now do the same compression pass on Chapters 15 and 16, but in your exact page style, meaning with your preferred paragraph length, section density, and how often you want cases named versus implied.

Chapter 17
Manifesto: Narrative is Capital

From a superficial view, capital markets appear to be a system of numbers. Valuation multiples, cash flow models, credit spreads, and regulatory ratios. These numbers evoke the image of objective, quantitative machines. Yet every number is an interpretation, every model is built on assumptions, every projection rests on confidence in what management discloses, and on what investors believe the company can deliver. Narrative sits at the center of that confidence.

Narrative is not window dressing. Narrative is not marketing. It functions as capital because it determines whether the numbers will be believed, whether models will converge, and whether investors will accept duration risk rather than demand a penalty for uncertainty. A company can have a strong balance sheet and still trade at a discount if the market cannot explain its economics with confidence. A company can have a compelling narrative and still trade at a discount if it cannot produce proof in audited results. The market pays up when narrative and numbers cohere, and when the company's capital plan can be underwritten with a lower required return.

17.1. Narrative as Financial Instrument

Accounting gave markets shared instruments for measurement. The income statement, the balance sheet, and the cash flow statement. Investors learned to read them, regulators codified standards, and credibility became scalable. Narrative serves an analogous function. It is the medium through which investors test assumptions, frame risk, and decide which variables should anchor the model.

A credible narrative reduces the cost of capital by compressing spreads, tightening the equity risk premium, and narrowing error bands in long-horizon cash flow and return models. An incoherent or implausible narrative widens, spreads, raises the required return, and extends the duration of valuation discounts. The market does not price narrative as words. It prices narrative as signal quality. The signal is measurable, and it is worth money.

17.2. Historical Perspectives

Markets have always priced narrative, even when they did not label it that way. In the nineteenth century, railroads raised capital through disclosed operating metrics such as route mileage, tonnage, and revenue per mile, alongside governance structures that made claims on cash flows credible. In the 1990s, many dot-com issuers sold disruption before proof, leading to valuations that could not survive once cash flows failed to materialize. In the 2010s, ESG frameworks became a credibility test. Sovereigns and corporates that adopted transparent, auditable disclosure attracted new pools of capital and compressed spreads. Those who staged ESG as rhetoric faced greenwashing accusations and valuation penalties.

The pattern is stable. What changes is the attribute of narrative that matters most. At different times, it has been governance, adoption, resilience, sustainability, or security. In every era, disciplined disclosure separated issuers that attracted capital from those that repelled it.

17.3. The Advisor's Duty

If narrative operates as capital, the advisor's role is not beautification. It is engineering. Advisory work is the design of scaffolding that enables investors to model, to test, and to allocate with confidence.

That duty is practical. Advisors inhibit overreach, impose disclosure discipline, and reconcile claims to proof. They engineer frameworks that remain credible under stress, including periods when operations are under duress. They anticipate activism, regulatory scrutiny, and reputational shocks. Above all, they treat narrative as inseparable from financials, because it changes the required return the market demands.

17.4. Narrative in a Time of Fragmentation

Narrative matters more now because information is fragmented across channels. Investors take cues not only from filings and calls, but also from social media, alternative data, enforcement actions, and political noise. Skepticism is pervasive. ESG has politicized certain disclosures. Activists and short sellers look for any discrepancy between what is said and what can be reconciled.

Under these conditions, consistency becomes a premium. Companies with disciplined disclosure frameworks, repeated cadence, and evidence that accumulates over quarters build durability. Companies that rely on hyperbole, omission, imprecision, or shifting definitions invite rumor, conjecture, and narrative arbitrage to set the price.

Narrative is not fully controllable. It is contestable. That contestability does not lessen its importance. It increases the premium on rigor.

17.5. Toward a New Standard

The market is moving toward higher expectations for disclosure architecture. Financial reporting is already codified. Adjacent disclosure regimes are expanding. ESG taxonomy is one starting point. Climate, cybersecurity, and governance disclosure requirements are others. Beyond regulation, practice must become more disciplined. Management teams and advisors must treat narrative with the same seriousness as capital allocation and risk governance.

Consider a future where disclosure architecture is evaluated with the same seriousness as financial reporting, where perception work becomes routine in select issuer categories, and where the credibility of disclosure is treated as an intangible asset that can be strengthened or impaired. The direction is clear. Issuers that anticipate the standard will enjoy an advantage in cost of capital, liquidity, and resilience.

17.6. Closing Manifesto

This book argues that capital markets advisory is architecture, not slogans. Credibility is produced through disciplined disclosure, analyst education, investor targeting, and credible governance. The variables differ by industry and business model, but the discipline is consistent. Tools make the discipline reproducible. Case studies show the cost of drift and the rewards of rigor.

The conclusion is simple. Narrative is capital. It determines whether numbers will be believed, whether liquidity will be attracted, and whether valuation can be defended through cycles. Companies that treat narrative as marketing will be discounted. Companies that treat narrative as capital will reduce their cost of capital and build durability. Advisors who understand this do not sell stories. They build the architecture of trust that allows capital to price the business fairly, and sometimes, to price it better than operations alone could justify in the moment.

Acronyms and Abbreviations

1. ADR - American Depositary Receipt
2. APAC - Asia Pacific
3. ARPU - Average revenue per user
4. ASC 606 - Accounting Standards Codification Topic 606 (Revenue from Contracts with Customers)
5. CAGR - Compound annual growth rate
6. CAPEX - Capital expenditures
7. CEO - Chief Executive Officer
8. CFO - Chief Financial Officer
9. DCF - Discounted cash flow
10. EBIT - Earnings before interest and taxes
11. EBITDA - Earnings before interest, taxes, depreciation and amortization
12. EGC - Emerging growth company
13. ESG - Environmental, Social and Governance
14. EV - Enterprise value
15. FCF - Free cash flow
16. FX - Foreign exchange
17. GAAP - Generally Accepted Accounting Principles
18. GDP - Gross domestic product
19. GP - General partner
20. ICFR - Internal control over financial reporting
21. IR - Investor relations
22. IRR - Internal rate of return

23. IPO / IPOs - Initial public offering / offerings
24. JOBS Act - Jumpstart Our Business Startups Act
25. KPI / KPIs - Key performance indicator(s)
26. LatAm - Latin America
27. LTV - Lifetime value
28. M&A - Mergers and acquisitions
29. MD&A - Management discussion and analysis
30. NAV - Net asset value
31. NDR / NDRs - Non deal roadshow(s)
32. NPV - Net present value
33. OPEX - Operating expenditures
34. PE – Private Equity
35. P&L - Profit and loss
36. P/E - Price to earnings ratio
37. Q1 - First quarter of the financial year
38. Q2 - Second quarter of the financial year
39. Q3 - Third quarter of the financial year
40. Q4 - Fourth quarter of the financial year
41. Reg S-K - Regulation S K (SEC regulation governing non financial statement disclosures)
42. Reg S-X - Regulation S X (SEC regulation governing form and content of financial statements)
43. ROA - Return on assets
44. ROE - Return on equity
45. ROIC - Return on invested capital
46. SaaS - Software as a service
47. SEC - U.S. Securities and Exchange Commission

48. SPAC / SPACs - Special purpose acquisition company / companies
49. SOTP - Sum of the parts (valuation)
50. TCV - Total contract value
51. TSR - Total shareholder return
52. U.S. - United States
53. VC - Venture capital
54. VIE - Variable interest entity
55. WACC - Weighted average cost of capital
56. YoY - Year over year

www.ingramcontent.com/pod-product-compliance
Lightning Source LLC
LaVergne TN
LVHW050914210926
848482LV00012B/439
* 9 7 9 8 2 9 5 4 8 3 5 7 8 *